GameStop

A Step by Step Guide to Financial Freedom

(How an Online Forum Shook Wall Street to Its Core)

Herbert Davis

Published By **Regina Loviusher**

Herbert Davis

GameStop: A Step by Step Guide to Financial Freedom (How an Online Forum Shook Wall Street to Its Core)

ISBN   978-1-77485-919-3

Legal & Disclaimer

The information contained in this ebook is not designed to replace or take the place of any form of medicine or professional medical advice. The information in this ebook has been provided for educational & entertainment purposes only.

The information contained in this book has been compiled from sources deemed reliable, and it is accurate to the best of the Author's knowledge; however, the Author cannot guarantee its accuracy and validity and cannot be held liable for any errors or omissions. Changes are periodically made to this book. You must consult your doctor or get professional medical advice before using any of the suggested remedies, techniques, or information in this book.

Upon using the information contained in this book, you agree to hold harmless the

Table Of Contents

Chapter 1: Scene Setting

What transpired in January 2021 was by far the most thrilling thing that happened following a year that was ravaged by a deadly pandemic. The public was in misinformation regarding what was actually taking place, and journalists did to explain the situation in a way that ordinary people could comprehend. Many of them offered interesting commentary that contributed to explaining what was going on. However, what people mainly got from this most was what they saw as the David as well as Goliath part of the dramathat lasted for the course of a week as if it was a lengthy duel. The fact that people were earning thousands of dollars while Wall Street titans were losing billions of dollars was a bittersweet rebuke for many who'd been feeling victimized of the market. To fully comprehend it we must learn something about the market. It will not bore you one cent, I guarantee. The action gets even more intense and full of more surprises when you see it in full-length. This is more than an explanation can do for you. Consider it as a an action plan.

How does the stock market function precisely?

It is helpful to take things a step further. Imagine that we have a company. It's doing well, however, we'd like to expand our company. There are several options of reinvesting our profits back into the company to expand it however, this could be difficult, or we could sell shares. Selling shares is similar to finding investors. Shares are a representation of ownership for a part of a business; this ownership may comprise profits as well as a company's assets. Shares offered on the market grant shareholders the right to profits, but without assets of the company. Shares are profitable by them since investors can sell them at a profit should they increase in value.

To us: We've purchased shares -- let's imagine 10,000 shares at 10 cents per share. Like this, we'll get an infusion of cash worth $100,000 into our company. We can utilize that cash to purchase new equipment and rent out more space, and hire highly skilled workers and anything else needed to expand our business, and generate income. As our company grows and our value increases, so does we see our value as our stock (those stocks we have sold) increases. Any investor looking to sell their shares realizes that they are highly valuable, and will only offer them for sale at what they consider to be an appropriate price. In the end, they are selling a stake in bigger profits. If we think that we are able to grow the business we could invest our profits in expanding our business until a certain time, we'll be able to grow enough and the marketplace will become too saturated to make growth not feasible. To ensure that investors are satisfied they can be paid parts of the profits. These are known as dividends. Businesses can pay all of the profits they earn to shareholders, or some of them and keep the rest to be used for other purposes. This is another reason which makes stock worth it It is possible to sell them to earn a profit as your business expands, or hold them for dividends or other rights.

However, the value of the stock may not always reflect the actual worth of a business. It doesn't need to. The price of stocks is demand and supply, despite the fact that shares represent ownership.

"Why?" you ask. Let me explain it this way If I have Tesla shares, there's no reason to stop me from getting up the next morning and trading them for $10 per share. It would be foolish man, but there's nothing that can stop me from doing so. I would be happy to purchase my shares. Everybody in the stock market is essentially trading. Sellers have posted bids, the prices they wish to purchase Tesla stocks at, and sellers are posting asking prices, the price they're willing to offer their stocks for. If sellers compete against each for the chance to sell their stock the stock, they reduce their prices to attract buyers to them. If enough sellers are doing this then the cost of the product will drop. If buyers compete with one another to purchase stocks, they will offer more and more expensive prices to purchase the stocks, pushing the price up.

The prices are correlated to the performance of the business however, they aren't the actual value of the company. The true value is what we would receive if we sold the assets of the business, like patents, property or other assets. The company's performance influences the value that the shares are sold at. If the company isn't doing well, investors are not keen to purchase these shares due to the fact that they might not be capable of selling them at an income, and the company may not be able to make dividends and, if the company chooses to purchase the shares back, they will not give a high price for the shares because the company isn't making as much money. Consider that. Sellers and buyers are both part of the company's performance since the business's performance may affect the public's interest for its shares and the happens to the shares.

Officially, the price of the stock market must reflect the worth of the business. This is exactly the way buyers and sellers do when they bargain. They are trying to find an acceptable price for their shares in the business. In the real world, these prices can be over or undervalue a business.

A customer could be able to say, "Look, I am not paying more than $10 for Tesla since their most recent earnings report indicates an increase in sales but a slight decrease."

A seller could state, "I have gone down by $20, and I'm not going to go any lower. You're just trying to purchase the shares for a reasonable price. Consider what they are spending on R&D. What are you telling me that buying these shares regardless of the most recent quarter, where unemployment is evidently high, isn't worth the price? I'm not kidding you!"

If sellers have enough fatigue, might be willing to accept "Okay but whatever, I will just take the shares. I've already made money anyway."

A few buyers might be more in need of a bargain. They are aware that Tesla is going to increase in price in price, and this could represent their final chance to purchase it at a bargain and say, "I will take it! If he's not willing to make an extra $10, I'll!"

The haggling takes place very fast often, thousands of times every second. The majority of traders do not participate in it , and instead buy the stock is at.

Depending on who is the most motivated, prices can fluctuate. However, everyone must be able to state that I am selling at this price, because it is evident that the company will be worth more. Why, though? I'm oversimplifying If Tesla were to be purchased it would be paid about the amount of the actual value of the company each share. Therefore, if the true worth of the company is $10 billion, and all shares added up were valued at $12 billion, the $10 billion spent to purchase Tesla would then be divided by the number of shares that the company holds. If the company is owned by 100,000 shares, that means shareholders would be an amount of 10,000 per share. That's a lot of money. The new owners could decide to not buy back shares. They may instead offer shareholders new shares in the company. They'll roughly cost the same.

The issue is how much a business costs in actual life is a factor that affects the price of its stock. This is the reason sooner or later, the prices of stocks that are overpriced or undervalued tend to be closer to and represent the value of what the actual value of the company. If investors decide to overvalue a business due to misinformation, hype or even deliberately. A few of those who promoted GameStop to their fans on YouTube were constantly talking about how the business was shifting its business model to be competitive on the internet. However, a quick look at the company's financials is troubling. For instance, in the last five years its debt has risen and its assets have declined and it's not able to reach its sales goals which means that earnings are declining. If investors want to believe in a magic that will allow the business to expand, they can purchase the shares. If enough investors believe that the value will increase even if there's no significant change in the business itself and the company's stock will rise. We'll watch how this unfolds with WallStreetBets.

When investors put aside funds to buy or sell stocks, they're betting. You purchase because you believe that the price will rise while you sell because you believe that it will not. The person who sells your shares will be betting on you and the buyer of your shares has a stake against your in general. There are many reasons investors could sell their shares, as it's not always clear what they are betting on, whether the stock will go up or down in the future. For example I may decide trade the shares of my Tesla stocks because I think I can find an investment that is attractive.

There are two ways to make money through stock investments: longing and shorting. The most obvious is the longing option. It's the process of buying shares at a cheaper price and then sell it for more when the value of the stock increases. Shorting occurs when you sell stock for a greater price and then buy it back at a lower cost and pocket the change.I can offer 100 shares of Tesla stock for just $100, thinking that the stock will drop in the event that the latest earnings report is released. If the earnings report is not great investors may decide to sell their shares and drive the price down. Let's say they drop to around $70. I could then purchase the shares at $70. I made $30 per share, by putting my money on the possibility that the price would drop. Short sellers don't need to own shares. Instead, they occasionally borrow them, and then sell them on the open market in the event that they believe that the share price of the company will decrease, and are charged a fee for borrowing. As with everything borrowed and returned, they must return the shares on an agreed time. Returning the shares means purchasing them back . This generally happens at the present prices.

Companies that are usually involved in short selling research the fundamentals of the business. They analyze what the company has and what it owes, as well as its revenue, cash flows, investment and debts and evaluate the market that the company operates in. In this way, they will assess if the price of its shares accurately reflect its actual value. If they find that the business is too expensive, they could anticipate that market prices will show that at some point or other. Therefore, they sell the company.

With advanced tools and models they are better in predicting whether this option is a great investment or not. Most of the time, they're right. If investors discover that the business they have invested in struggling, they are forced to sell. Those purchasing don't want to purchase shares at a price they feel aren't worth the company and prices drop.

However, short selling is extremely risky. If the stock is up it will cost you your money. There is no limit on the height that the stock can rise, and that's the issue. When the stock is down it will have an upper limit. When it is at zero, it's over. If it increases it could theoretically last forever. This is why investment companies take their time when assessing the situation prior to they make a short sale on the stock.

Think about this: you loan one hundred pieces of Tesla stocks for $10,000. You're certain that the price is going to fall due to reasons. You decide to sell those shares at a value of $662. You will receive the sum of $66,200 in your account. The stock is waiting to decline so you can purchase it and earn profits. The stock continues to fall slow, but eventually getting to $600. You are convinced that it will continue to fall, so you decide not to buy it back. One day you awake to find that Tesla has perfected autonomic vehicle technology to the fullest extent. That's right! It is now possible to get in one of these vehicles and it's capable of driving on any traffic or road and is more secure than driving. This is the ultimate goal of self-driving vehicles. In a flash, Tesla stock goes up by $1000, as investors vie to join in the fun. This shares are now valued at $1600 per share.

You must purchase that back. It's going to be $160,000. You've already suffered a loss of more than $100,000 through this trade. If the price rises and you put off longer, the more you'll need to shell out to return the shares back to their owners. This is how risky short selling could be.

Melvin Capital and Citron Capital have made the right decision about GameStop and attempted to make a gain from the company's inevitable demise. They looked at and modelled every kind of risk. This is the way that investment firms do, and this was among the most rational decisions to take. Actually the opposite is, well, foolish. But there's a variable that they didn't consider: WallStreetBets. Who would think of including an online forum like Reddit forum into their models?

Chapter 2: Democraticization? Yes!

The small guy was always outgunned. He was not able to compete. could match the bigger guys. Individual investors don't have the same resources as institutional investors do, even with tools and trading platforms. If you'd like to be a part in the market for financial instruments, there are two options to do it: either through the traditional broker or a discount broker.

Brokers are middlemen who bring together buyers and sellers for financial products. They also offer a variety of financial services for investors. They will provide you with money to trade the example of. When you purchase or sell stocks, you'd be doing the transaction through their. Traditional brokers are costly. They conduct in-depth research, offer financial guidance specific to meet your needs and employ their sophisticated tools to help make more money for your account. These brokers are in close contact with their clients. They contact them regarding trading opportunities, offer their trades, and rely on their own expertise to provide an understanding to their trading. In short they're the ideal choice. There's only one caveat you must be rich to be able to afford these.

To get a bank account at their bank, you have to make a minimum deposit of six figures into the account. They charge anywhere from $10 to $20 for each trade, and sometimes require an annual charge that ranges from 1 to 2 percent of the funds they hold for you. It's not necessary to worry about not being rewarded enough to assist you, because the moment you earn money, they earn profits, and their whole arsenal is available to you.

On the other hand discount brokers provide their clients the data they've devised as well as the trading software and many other tools. However, their customers must understand it all on their own and decide how to invest as they want to. It's a lot and, when in this situation it is likely that you lack the knowledge and expertise the brokers do, and therefore can be susceptible to making mistakes or not comprehending the motivation of numbers that could be frightening, but should not be taken too seriously. It's not as bad, but you are disadvantageed, but you can access top software and top-quality research by the most reputable. The cost is a bit lower however, you'll still require a little bit of cash to take part. However, the fees are very high for ordinary people like us. If you aren't convinced check out sites such as StockBrokers.com.

Trading, in other words, is costly. Even if it weren't so expensive, it's extremely difficult to compete against an entire room of experts research, insiders, as well as stock analysts. Although a lot of information on these companies is readily available but you aren't able to compete. Individual investors, also known as"retail investors," are often referred to "dumb cash" and the players from institutions are referred to as "smart money." This is due to the fact that smart money is smart in their decisions made with money. They know when it is time to move into positions or hold, sell or perform whatever. Although dumb money is susceptible to make a variety of unintentional errors, it is also susceptible to failing to make the right decisions at any moment, they are merely creatures of fate.

What kind of errors does reckless money make? They make trades in a rush and ignore the fundamentals because headlines say the opposite. They are prone to being influenced by headlines, and they might not have that much impact on the performance of the price of shares. They frequently fall victim to FOMO by rushing to buy shares as everyone else is buying them. They believe that if they wait they'll miss out. They aren't aware that this is often a way to drive prices up without justification. This is the way that bubbles begin. They are based on forecasts of the way the market will function rather than how the company itself is doing. This is a major mistake since prices can be prone to being closer to the actual worth of the company. They tend to sell before the market opens or enter in positions during the most inconvenient timings. They aren't able to access the most recent breaking news or high-speed data, and so they buy items at prices that aren't Smart money can take advantage of that by trading with seemingly the most attractive prices, but knowing that prices aren't based on actual data (Spacey 2021).

My argument? The dumb money isn't disadvantaged but smart money enjoys making use of these opportunities wherever they are able to. You can imagine the reactions from smart money when applications such as Robinhood were introduced. This was not only welcomed, but it was celebrated. Are you looking to make finance more democratic? Oh yes, do it.

The more naive money swimming with sharks that are big will mean increased food supply for those big fish. The idea of an app such as Robinhood making finance more accessible so that everyone can have a an opportunity to participate in the market was attractive to clients for a reason: it was affordable and had no commission fees and other expenses, meaning there was no obstacle. Stocks offer a great chance to make profits. What number of people can afford to invest?

On Robinhood's website it states that when the company's founders sold the software they developed in the early 1990s to Wall Street hedge funds, "they realized that large Wall Street firms were paying virtually nothing to trade stocks and the vast majority of Americans were being charged commissions for every trade. The founders made a decision to change that and returned to California to develop a financial service that would give everyone--not only the rich to access the financial markets" (About Us, n.d.). It is more likely that they saw a different method of earning money for them and for the big players.

When you learn how Robinhood makes money, it is difficult to believe the we-are-here-for-the-little-guy branding of Robinhood. One of the ways Robinhood earns money is through the payment of orders flow. It is because market makers are paying Robinhood to handle the orders that their clients make. Market makers typically are banks or other financial institutions that help keep the markets moving with cash , so that transactions can occur in a short time.

Market makers pay to handle the orders so that they can locate the best deal to handle their orders and earn the profit they receive by the transaction. They achieve this by buying and selling the shares themselves however at a certain price. Do you want to sell? They purchase from you. Do you want to purchase? They will sell it to you. Based on this which are the true clients of Robinhood? Are they the small guy that pays no fee or are the market makers that pay them to process their orders? Robinhood reaps the benefits of high-frequency trading. I do not know about you but I think the most important customers are those institutions. They're not even beginning to consider the real-time data these types of agreements offer to these institutions.

Naturally they're thrilled with the opening up of finance to the public, since it means that more Americans are willing to trade and, in turn, generate increased profits for their customers. Since its debut in 2013 Robinhood has made trading more popular. The site now has over 20 million customers. It's not that I believe trading is bad, but I am saying that the inequality makes it risky and Robinhood's portrayal of themselves in the role of Robin Hood is a bit of a prank.

If big investors are able to hold private meetings with corporations while we don't be aware of what's discussed, we shouldn't expect the game for fairness. Smart money is connected to large investors, which means they have access to information which the rest of us aren't until it's late. High-speed trading is always better for the common man simply because they are equipped with advanced tools, access and resources (Sorkin and co. 2021).

So, how can the little guy do it?

Chapter 3: The Inception

The year 2012 was when Jaime Rogozinski was working for Inter-American Bank as IT support. At the time of his life He was single and had an abundance of disposable income and he decided to put it into investments (Brown 2021). You are aware of how a certain kind of money could be. It's a constant whirlwind, and demands for something completed with it. But spending recklessly wasn't in his thoughts, at least not following the lessons learned in the last decade.

The world was just beginning to crawl from recession following the financial crash of Lehman Brothers that led to the Great Recession. He was among the very few generation of people who had what people would consider to be an "good work." He had witnessed protests like Occupy Wall Street condemning the injustice and moral inequity of the 1 percent.

It's not surprising that Rogozinski became interested in the financial markets. In his view the financial markets were casinos only for the rich with stakes significantly higher, and everyone else was ostracized from participating. According to him that, people on Wall Street displayed the same sort of reckless behavior that as you would see when you visit Las Vegas. They concealed all this under bizarre financial instruments, the use of acronyms and market magic. There was no one but one to feel this way regarding the markets. The confidence to Wall Street had plummeted among the public at large. The market meant for financing business changed to become something entirely different. They were betting on themselves, making extremely risky bets with the potential to harm all, and the majority of public did not have a say in the situation. Rogozinski wasn't a savior. He looked at the situation and he wanted to be part in the game. If they're going participate in this game, then we might be able to join in the game, making this more democratic. If you are unable to beat them, join them.

Rogozinski describes looking for investment advice only to get the same advice that all best financial advisors would tell their clients: "Invest in index funds and dividend stocks." They are usually secure, stable and reliable. However, they do have one issue they are not very rewarding and require an extended time to grow. Returns are typically low. In a time of the burden of high student debt, a the high cost of living and stagnant income it didn't seem feasible to make this investment and then expect to live to retirement. It's a lot of effort and time, but If you had money enough, you could invest in this way. Average returns from an index fund average around 7% per annum.

If the financial state of your life is similar this, it's almost impossible to keep track of your finances. We are overwhelmed by hopelessness and recklessness. Furthermore, you're youthful and full of energy You're looking for something more exciting, something which could be life-changing. High risk, but high reward isn't it? You're looking to be as confident and as petty as the big players on Wall Street. Diversify? Yes, but don't attempt to make it appear like Wall Street isn't just a sophisticated casino equipped with the latest tools, a place that could earn millions or thousands of dollars within a matter of weeks. You're looking to join "the most exclusive table of poker" (Brown 2021) around the globe. The boomer advice on investing from the past would not work now!

When Rogozinski searched online for forums that could assist the situation, all he could find were long-term conservative strategies for investing. This was not appealing at all. He wanted to connect with like-minded individuals open to exchanging aggressive investing strategies that were both short-term with high returns (Garg 2021). Therefore, he started WallStreetBets via Reddit.

WallStreetBets started to grow steadily with the rise of apps that do not charge commissions such as Robinhood (Rogozinski 2020). If you examine the graphs, you'll observe a surprising correlation and in fact the most popular trading application with a lot of customers using WallStreetBets are Robinhood. If you take a look at WallStreetBets growth in subscribers it's very constant and predictable over the first five years. The number of subscribers increases from 1,500 in the initial year, to around 100 thousand in 2017. After 2017 the number of subscribers had increased by more than a third. As 2018 came to an end the number nearly doubled to 450,000. By the end of 2019, the number was 7722,000 subscribers. It would require the pandemic to really propel the numbers.

The rise of WallStreetBets is attributable to the rise of trading apps. We have spoken about it as well, however, an expansion of financial instruments that allow users to hedge their risks and make more sophisticated bets was one of the reasons (Rogozinski 2020). The more financial instruments that are added to those platforms, the greater methods of earning money are developed with some being more exciting than others. There are more games that are included in the casinos, in a sense. Alongside this, there was an increase in YouTube channel, book and traders, some of whom were on WallStreetBets.

These factors all work to increase the amount of trading available to the general public, but it is the pandemic that would accelerate things further. The lockdown was in place within New York, and the pandemic was officially afoot within the United States, the New York Times as well as other large publications featured on the front page of their websites on their website, a graph of Dow Jones falling. In the week following it was the week that it was reported that the Dow Jones fell to its lowest level since its peak in the Great Recession. It is possible that you be able to recall this. It was all over the place. The loss of trillions of dollars was widespread because of layoffs. off and the economy was slowed to a standstill. It appeared as if Wall Street and the economy was interconnected.

Then something remarkable happened that lasted for a long time: the economy was getting worse, while the market rose to record highs. There's been no clearer method of showing how disengaged Wall Street is from the economy. This is in spite of the fact that certain tech companies were performing very well in the pandemic -- in actuality, because of it, but this didn't explain all the activities happening on the market.

A lot of people were in their homes, with virtually nothing to do. They spent lots of time on the internet, and a portion of the period was spent in the process of thinking about ways to earn money, and experimenting. When they heard that the market was seeing improved times They must have wondered, "How do I get involved?" Then that Super Bowl Robinhood commercial came to the forefront of their minds. It says, "You don't need to become an investor. You're already one!"

In 2020, the amount of members to WallStreetBets was up by a million and a couple of thousand. In the eye of Wall Street and financial journalists alike, WallStreetBets was a quirky group of investors who went there for losses if they were looking bet on losing their money. It was insidious, extreme and loud, rude and awash with bro-code. The people made thousands, sure. However, people also lost thousands. It's funny, they were both widely praised. WallStreetBets were a meme that reduced the seriousness of markets and turned them into a mere game. This same mindset that has made them the dark sheep of the market was also their strength, as they could see markets differently, which made the mainstream uncomfortable, but they were nevertheless true to the essence of what Wall Street was and what it was since the beginning.

To understand the various ways WallStreetBets have mutated Wall Street, you need to examine their culture. The subreddit celebrates both losses and wins. It is a reference to risky transactions as YOLO. YOLO can be used both as a verb and a noun. It is possible to YOLO the stock you own that means you are entering an extremely risky investment because you live only once (Brown 2021, Brown). Why is that? They refer to the profits from trades that are successful as tendies and refer to stocks that lose money as stainings (although they didn't invent terms like stonks). They are known as loss porn. which is when they are able to share their losses with applause. This kind of language is a way of gamifying Wall Street, removing the complete impact of what would otherwise be a negative situation. Another thing occurs in this setting as well; there's an intimateness, a connection which creates a community helping people feel less lonely and connected to something everyone else simply isn't.

However, WallStreetBets isn't intended for all players. Perhaps that's the reason. There is no room for political correctness or sanity on the subreddit. Disgusting content and hateful speech is like a river that flows through the countless memes about finance. They create memes that both offend and provide a description of the financial market. You'd think there'd be some sort of difference, but that they have a common goal with all people, similar to South Park. This kind of humor is a source of irritation. Rogozinski refers to WallStreetBets ' Reddi as "equal opportunities insulters"(2020). It's not hard to laugh at times when you hear this, right? What's that?

This is exactly the kind of reaction the chaos of WallStreetBets community provokes for those who aren't familiar in a mix of bemusement as well as confusion, disbelief and occasionally, offence.

On January 1, 2019, the Rogozinski family was disqualified of moderating the reddit after the rules of Reddit prohibit moderators from selling their services to communities they manage. The subreddit which owed so much to him has disowned him and they do not wish being associated with his work again. In some instances they do not want to attribute him to the creation of WallStreetBets. The rage and hatred they feel towards him is visible on the subreddit as well as in all his appearances on YouTube. I'll provide a sample of various comments

This person is banned from Wsb. Don't listen to him, he's not a representative of that subreddit.--Owen Kramer (2021)

THIS GUY IS A SELL OUT WHO NO LONGER REPRESENTS THE WSB COMMUNITY.-- Dominik Seitz (2021)

He was dismissed. He didn't resign from his role of moderating duties.--Evan (2021)

This guy had nothing to do with be associated in WSB for forever.--narfie (2021)

He didn't "step away." He was banned from his own forum for trying to monetize it.--SweetenessPlaysGames (2021)

This is a fraud! He didn't invent WSB! He was a fake who came up and got the spotlight! Check your sources PLEASE!--Anton Yatsenko (2021)

The comments continue in and out, which are being variations of the exact trolling and attempting to denigrate the person. This is the way they view the movement as a whole, if you want to call them as such.

Prior to the time Rogozinski was gone the company, there had been some changes taking place at WallStreetBets. Although the vast majority of the time spent on WallStreetBets regardless of the memes and financial porn, is engaging in discussions about stock and companies however, another trend was beginning to take shape: a trend to pool money into specific stocks. If an investment idea was well-known, the majority of the community jumped to it.

Chapter 4: The Rise Of The Memers

The impact that communities such as WallStreetBets influence the world of trading is immense and should not be undervalued. There are individuals on the subreddit who have significant followings and influence beyond the subreddit community. They can also transfer opinions of the subreddit to an audience that is larger, usually using methods that may be more easy to accept for the wider community that isn't able to cope with anything similar to the chaos of WallStreetBets. A good example of how reckless opinions impacted the public at large is through meme stocks. GameStop serves as an illustration of a meme-related stock.

Meme stocks are ones that are, for better or worse are a little like memes. That means they circulate around infectively expanding for those "in in." This usually includes individuals who are young and investing on trading platforms like Robinhood. The people who buy meme stocks don't buy them because of the company's core values (that is market-speak for value/performance) (Witty 2020). They do it in order to show their worth that they are funny or wacky. This is why they're often viewed as risky and overpriced investments that can swing widely according to how fashionable they are at that specific moment in the lives of those who participate in buying the stocks. It is possible to earn money through the meme stock market, but the value is mostly tied to the mood of traders.

When you buy memes generally, there's a storyline that is associated with it (Witty 2020). A narrative that all, or at the least, the majority of those who are participating enjoys or thinks is interesting. The word meme also refers to an obsession on being casual and enjoying the moment. It's odd to place fun and money together however that's precisely what we're seeing here. There's an advantage to playing around with money but not taking it seriously as trading can be difficult, and if you decide to take the game seriously, as it is recommended that you do take it, you could end up becoming more emotional than best for your health. It could lead you to make decisions which are not rational and detrimental in the end. However, if the motive comes from fear, then it can be advantageous in the event that you are trying to avoid losing money as your aim. If you are obsessed with the possibility of not losing any money that's what you'll be good at. It is impossible to get more proficient at earning money. Making money involves making a decision, testing methods, as well as learning how to make things easier so you're able to be more impartial.

The problem is that this reckless attitude can make people more naive regarding their finances, possibly falling into financial danger. There's something to this notion. If something appears to be something that everyone else is playing, then people can reduce the risk of the game, even if the game is extremely risky. We don't mean that we're lemmings. We're not, but we do behave in ways that aren't particularly beneficial due to the fact that we have taken refuge in the safety and security of social cohesion. We think we're all on the same side. It's a weird notion considering that we're not taking on the risk together. We're not in the same way and some of us -- the sheep in sheep's clothes to be precise --will come out of the situation better.

What am I talking about? The cynicism that is inherent to meme stock. One is that we're an individualistic society and the money offered by the investors is theirs for the taking and doesn't belong to any group, which includes the profits or losses (as I have mentioned earlier). Second, meme stocks defy the idea of markets reflecting the value of a company. Nobody believes that the value of stocks is real however, they do believe they do or are a representation of something though the market is governed by forces, and a snarkiness that says, "Not necessarily."

The fact that those limits are able to be stretched and altered by those who invest, the smart money or dumb money, exposes the game for an actual tool that can be utilized to make cash by defrauding those who are less skilled. It's not exactly like the magician's hat but it's pretty close. Like magic, everyone is aware of how the trick works. Now , they're looking to see whether they can "out tricks" one another to the tune of millions.

It's very cynical. But this is what it appears like.

Meme stocks are not a good investment for large investors or for those who aren't involved in the meme market. There are many new investors and experienced investors who may buy stock because they think there is something positive happening at the company. However, to them they are investing in an empty meme stock that is bound to plummet once the excitement fades.

When you see stock prices rising within a year or two may be right to conclude that something exciting is happening with the business, and the company may be a promising investment for the future. No one would advise investing in a business based on information from two years ago or more, and a lack of knowledge of the product it creates, or a proper market analysis, or even industry analysis. However, they do. They're not stupid. The stock market mania of memes is powerful and persuasive. Are you saying that you haven't thought of investing a few hundred dollars to purchase GameStop just for fun? I'm sure I did. It's tempting. But , the majority of investors aren't sure what's happening and invest believing the price will increase. They are, however, stock that is overpriced. If you're savvy and have the right mindset, you could make profits, but that will need to be aware of what's happening so that you can be able to enter and exit at the right time. In their individual manner, the meme stock added an additional risk that investors, big and small should be aware of when investing.

Imagine this scenario: You've got an additional $2,000. You don't want it to be unproductive, so that you should place it into stocks. In the end, you're hearing about the company A making good progress in the marketplace. There's plenty of buzz about it, and it's predicted to expand. This is the message that everyone is sharing on their timelines, however. There are stories of children who have put up $1,000 and transformed it into $20,000 after investing their money in a short-term stocks. You see these images of people who've earned some money by getting involved in the same market. The suits are affirming that the investment is not smart, but then the anchor on that news program was questioning an executive from a hedge fund about his bias against small investors. You think that maybe this time, it's OK to invest in company A. It has only begun to expand since the whole issue was a big draw for you So surely it will. You put all your money into it and then watch as the price rises by 10 percent. You're ecstatic. You're amazed to discover that it's actually working so you decide to hang on for a while. After a couple of days everybody sells since they don't have the money to keep increasing prices and the stock goes down by 60 percent. You've lost a significant amount of cash.

This is a lot more likely for couples close to retirement, for instance.

In less eloquent terms meme stocks can be described as minefields for people who aren't interested in them. However, in the year 2020 the risks posed by meme stocks was hardly any and that's why the usual business method that is the norm on Wall Street.

I have stated that meme stocks are a way to expose Wall Street as a trick factory in which stocks are separated from the actual value of businesses. But the old suits of Wall Street are half right in their rejection of that notion. Investors buy stocks because they are valuable because of what the company's doing. They aren't just playing the market. It is because the majority of the investors whether institutional or private, are invested in the businesses they invest in and they are looking to profit from their investment performance. Meme stock mania is an unintentional game that is just a portion of the market, yet it is able to bring a lot of sadness and happiness. Yes, stocks can be overvalued or undervalued, but they tend to be hung around the actual worth of the company due to the fact that this is what the market wants.

Chapter 5: The Business As Usual

Short sellers are a mystery that lurk on Wall Street. They make bets on the performance of businesses. They claim, "Oh, we think Tesla will perform badly in the coming year, therefore we'll sell the company." Sellers of short positions take stock on loan, then they sell it, then take it back for the lower cost and keep the profit.

If you've not noticed, let me show the moral ambiguity of of this. Imagine you are searching for a vehicle to purchase. You meet a car owner who would like to sell his car for $20,000. The car is checked out, and everything appears good, so you decide to purchase it. Six months later, the car is down significantly in value and you don't think you've been thrilled with it. It's been a bit of problem. The car owner is back to say, "Hey, let me take it off your shoulders. I'll pay you 10,000 to take it." Now you're feeling pretty content. You'll accept anything as not only has your car decreased in value, but it's quite a challenge to complete.

"Thank Thank you!" you say profusely when you sign documents, after which $10,000 will be wired to your account.

It turns out that the owner of the car had borrowed the vehicle (let's suppose it's legal) and was aware from extensive study that the car was likely to decline its value. So they figured they could earn an easy buck by selling the vehicle to someone else before it appreciated and then purchased it back returning it to the original owner.

You'd feel like you've been cheated and cheated by. Do I have it right? is it me? They've stolen your money. I'm sure that you'd investigate if there's any legal procedure that you could follow. The issue with stocks and short sales is the fact that an option like that doesn't exist. It is legal.

Based on this, you can imagine why people be ambivalent about or dislike short sellers. Keep in mind that short sellers do not know how much the value of the stock will decrease. They evaluate the performance of a company, then look at the performance of the company, and then determine that it is overvalued. The price of the company will decrease as investors realize the reality. It is what happens most of the time. On the stock market there are many companies that are overvalued than those with a low value. Therefore, it's tempting to short-sell those shares. In addition, short sellers face substantial risk, and theoretically infinite risk. They are able to hedge their risk through other financial instruments however, they are highly vulnerable. We've discussed this: Prices could drop to zero, however they can increase to an infinite level when they locate the perfect fuel source. Perhaps the risk they take will make us see that short sales are Wall Street's most extreme sport. The only risk is the cost and the excitement.

Warren Buffet, arguably the most successful investor of all time dislikes short selling. Buffet relates how it caused havoc to the lives of people he has known, leaving them in financial ruin (Forberg 2021). This shows the kind of bet this is. However, short selling can be attractive because lots of money could be made through it. It is because companies who are failing are obvious if you're equipped with the proper knowledge or knowledge.

Short sellers conduct research and study companies. They identify a company they're fairly certain is going to fall and place the bet through short selling it. If they're proven to be wrong, the results could be devastating. One of the largest Short sellers that were in industry was Melvin Capital and Citron Capital.

In the year 2018 Melvin Capital did the unthinkable and sold 0.8 percent of Nintendo stock, despite being aware that the sales had increased due of the Switch. It's no secret that the Switch is a big hit and not just as an item to market however, but also as a product that consumers love making use of. Furthermore, 0.8 percent doesn't seem like a lot but it's 1.2 million shares. In the light of such a good picture it's not surprising it was Melvin Capital was operating this way. Nintendo appeared to be as solid an organization as any however, its stock was slipping. When asked about the reason for selling Nintendo, Gabriel Plotkin, director of the fund declined to comment, and instead upped the stakes. Plotkin already had established himself as a renowned investor by doing this. Melvin Capital launched in December of 2014, and during its initial year, it grew by 47% and landed at the second position on Bloomberg's hedge fund ranking. Melvin Capital was the rock star of the moment (Nakamura and the 2018).

If a large institutional investor sells short an organization that's doing good on paper it can be confusing to the people who watch. What can they learn that we do not know? You'll be pleased to find out that Nintendo stock is now upwards, however, looking back, you'll be able to see the decline. How much did Melvin Capital bet? $400 million. We're not sure how long Plotkin kept his decision however, we do know they had a short position until July. The price of shares of Nintendo fell throughout the year. It began to show signs of recovery towards the beginning of 2019.

How did they find out? Why did they take this wager? We don't knowfor sure, but it seems like they were right and received their dollars' worth. This is just a demonstration of the intelligence of hedge funds as well as their arsenal of tools they possess that allows them to take a risk that seems counterintuitive and yet reap the benefits. It's amazing. The hedge funds that are like this require a lot of research. They visit the business and talk to people at the company and try to gain an idea about how the business is running. This is why their investments are important to investors of all sizes. They transmit a message.

Citron Capital was another big name in the world of hedge funds and its chief Andrew Left was already a famous short seller and extremely proficient at it. In the New York Times feature, Left was referred to as "the Bounty Hunter of Wall Street." Another aspect he was famous in is Citron Research, a website which "offered opinions about Wall Street," having published more than 150 articles known for their ability to spot fraudulent practices and bad business practices (Left, n.d.). They would release reports, usually accusing businesses of fraud, poor fundamentals, or abuse, and finally, some (Left, n.d.). Citron Research functions to expose and expose dubious investments. They have stated that they've never wanted to participate with "gotcha journalistic practice" (Left, n.d.) But that's the way it's usually presented and I'm not convinced it's a good thing. Their work can benefit investors.

The results of all this research are short-selling concepts. Most often, Left places bets against the companies he writes about and has had a lot of success in the process. Short-selling and reports cause a lot of resentment from the people they target as well as the person was sued several times, yet He has not been unsuccessful in a court case at his native United States. He has a phrase that he uses: "I stand by my investigation. For me, it's been a blessing that I've been more correct as opposed to mistaken" (2015).

It's hard to find more awesome than this. The quote is from an Wall Street Journal piece, The "Short" Who took Valeant Stock.

The Left accused Valeant of writing fraudulent invoices, and compared them to Enron. While there is no doubt about the benefits of identifying uncovering fraud for investors, we shouldn't assume that Left does not profit from this kind of media. It is possible that he is the largest benefit. The accusations he makes have the potential of speeding up the decline of the stock. It may sound suspicious, but as long as the information he claims isn't fabricated and he is able to openly admit this. We'll get to these strategies later. To be clear, Valeant stock fell by over 90% from the peak of August 2015. The following month the its CEO J. Michael Pearson resigned.

This is only one of many events in the many other events Left has been involved in.

Since short-selling is more risky, businesses who conduct it must be very cautious about it. Many resources are put to ensure that they're cautious. At the time it was a mystery about the likelihood that Melvin Capital and Citron Capital two giants of Wall Street, would be destroyed by Redditors using the smartphone application with a humorous name. They knew their business very well and knew how to do it.

Chapter 6: Birth Of Villains

The best interests for the seller to allow the price to decrease. The market, generally is on the upswing. It is upwards and upwards. It has been that way since the beginning of time. In the event of a recession or depression, it is only temporary. Therefore, short selling is kind of contrary to the trend. Take Nintendofor instance: It was down for about 8 months before it started to rise again. The price has since risen even during the midst of the pandemic. The price of the shares is close to the level is was, when it reached its peak prior to that Great Recession.

Some short sellers are involved in what's known as short and distortion. It is when traders embark to the extreme of a smear operation using rumors, fake information and fear to push the price of a specific stock lower (Chen, n.d.). They might say things such as, "The company's finances are unstable, and investors need to get out when they have the chance to."

They are extremely focused on the discrediting of and fighting against any person who isn't in their favor. These kinds of scenarios typically get very intense. After they've successfully created doubt or created confusion The stock will usually go down since investors don't know the implications of it , and are looking to sell their stock in order to protect themselves.

The panic causes that scenario that we all have experienced. It's like when you are walking down the street, and suddenly you see a man sprinting towards you screaming in fear or fleeing from something. Even if it's hard to see and aren't sure what they're running from, you are unable to be able to resist the urge to stop at a stop or join them. The market's volatility can have similar effects. There are people who sell their shares, and then you think, "I should, right? The financials are in order But why is the price falling? What is the reason for selling? Do they have knowledge that I do not? I'm not sure what's happening however, I need to go I guess?"

Then, your friend remarks, "Yeah, I heard horrible reports about these people. It seems like they cooked their books or did something else."

"What? Are you really serious?" you ask, stunned.

"Yeah."

"Where did you get this information? I've not heard anything about it in or in the media."

"It's all on across the Internet." It's all over the internet. take out their phones and show you a forums or tweets that you aren't able to verify however, they're all to be pretty authentic. There are debunkers that go over the top to calm investors however, there are influencers of the trade who claim to speak as if they've discovered an insider's knowledge and are encouraging their followers to sell the shares.

Whatever the case, whether right or right The well is poisoned and it becomes challenging to persuade yourself to stick with the market because there's something funny taking place. In the end, that's all you need to do to decisions. Even if the business came out to dispel the rumors of poor performance or bad financials, it will automatically become negative news: "Why are they going to this extent to deny these rumors even if they don't have any credibility to the stories at all?"

Good news is not always good news is what seems to work best to Wall Street. But, the fact it's in the interests for companies to show themselves in the most positive possible light to shareholders makes it difficult to be able to trust them at times. They often minimize negative aspects, and focus on positive ones and then burying negatives to the side. Some companies have made this mistake. They'll do whatever it takes in order to make you believe that things are right or that things will improve even when their own self-confidence is waning. When despair takes hold the focus is on keeping employees and investors "happy" and hoping that things will change.

In the end, the Chief Executive Officer of Lehman Brothers, Richard Fuld the employees in the eyes and said "Every person in your team must be proud and confident. The company is strong today, and we'll emerge more resolute. We've done it before and we'll repeat the feat." Twelve months after the collapse of the bank, it was a complete disaster (Smith 2009). A CEO who gives an address of assurance such as this can be a negative signal for the future.

In the meantime, short sellers are accumulating their gains with every investor who sells their shares because of falsehoods and rumors. If the rumors prove true and it becomes clear that everything was in order with the company for a long time the short sellers purchased back stock and earned plenty of money. This is how it works.

What's the reason? because our faith with the established has diminished. Anyone who was critical of the purchase by GameStop as well as any bad information regarding GameStop was considered to be an apologist for short-sellers or a villain. Short selling is not a good reputation because it has a dark side , due to its tendency to adopt the terrible tactics we've previously described. If someone is made to feel like a victim and criticized, it's easy to wish they fall short. This was one of the motivational factors for customers who bought into GameStop during the craze short seller bad. Buyers are good.

When you worked as a reporter, analyst who was expressing displeasure at the absurdity of the GameStop fanfare It was difficult to keep from being criticized- that's what I'm saying. What was going on with GameStop was intriguing however, it was anything other than innocent. We'll talk more about this.

In the eyes of the general public short sellers were viewed as criminals, which made WallStreetBets the good guys, or so it seemed.

Chapter 7: The Case Of Gamestop

The question of whether or not GameStop is a great investment has been among the hot issues. A lot of investors believed that they weren't, and a lot of investors were looking to sell its shares rather than purchasing the shares. Many hours of research and analysis was involved in those choices; we've observed how hard institutional investors are when deciding whether which company to short. There were some who believed GameStop stood a good chance of rebounding should the new management make the appropriate decisions in the next few years.

The arguments against GameStop were not many but were strong such as falling sales, a rising debt ratios, and a drop in earnings and assets. The company was operating what was considered to be an ailing business by selling physical copies of consoles, games and other games in a brick-and mortar store, as the world transitioned to games delivered online and some customers had never even seen the physical version of a game, and the majority all items can be shipped overnight. The company was trying to expand into other market segments, but it was not a success the company retreated and remained focused on gamers, which was the primary customer base. Certain worries were legitimate but some were exaggerated. (I am excluding GameStop's online store as it's not the largest part of its business.)

The company's success was mostly contingent on what it could or do, and they had some fantastic ideas for investors and many of them seemed like they could be viable. In the early days, GameStop had a market capitalization at $260 million (its total value in the stock market) and shares were trading at $4. The reason was that it was a simple gamble to take due to the fact that GameStop was so affordable. If you didn't win then it wasn't a major deal, it was only $4. If it was correct, then you could have made quite a bit of money. This is the type of thing that even small investors want to hear: a cheap risky investment that can yield huge. There are a number of positive reasons to place this bet, as we'll see them explained by expert Scott Preston, GameStop itself and also famousized by YouTube trading guru Keith Gill, also known as Roaring Kitty.

Gill is believed to have laid the the foundations for what would later turn into the GameStop buying fanfare. Through a YouTube video of one hour as well as a few TikToks Gill is believed to have made the most convincing arguments in favor of buying into GameStop. Many traders who followed his lead began to replicate and propagate his ideas, which was to become the excitement we witnessed in January. Gill was thorough You can tell the amount of letters, reports to investors, news articles and peer-reviewed research on investment that was then compiled into a coherent presentation that viewers could easily read and comprehend. Gill had the added benefit of a more casual and likable appearance that many social media influencers possess.

So let's take a look at some of the ideas the GameStop pro-gamers came up with that made GameStop the fav among small investors. They also helped make him a millionaire.

Physical Games are Still Big

Contrary to what you've been told that physical games are huge. I'm sure that the delivery of digital media is huge however, the number of physical games are far higher than those of digital games. This is the reason why Sony and Microsoft continue to produce consoles equipped with optical drives. The game industry would not accept the complete transition to digital delivery until they saw the numbers change. Physical discs are falling in value and the idea that they're an old-fashioned thing is simply untrue (Preston 2020). If you're a fan of games likely to have seen this, such as the way your friend still purchases the latest FIFA disc, instead of buying a digital copy of it and download it to their computer. There is a choice however, not many people will take it. So, GameStop can still survive.

This is just one of the factors that make up a portion of the whole picture however, by itself it's not an effective argument for short sellers such as Gabriel Plotkin and Andrew

Left. Physical copies of games are still in high demand as are books, but who's to say that the consumer would want to purchase the books at GameStop? There are other sellers both on the internet and in the physical store, that perform the same task with the same efficiency. GameStop claims to have around 60 million satisfied customers who are part of the PowerUp Rewards program. perhaps that's enough incentive for them to stick in the business. But do you really be able to count on?

Generation Y likes experiences and GameStop is a Good Place to Serve Them

There is a common belief that millennials are more interested in experiences than things. It's true. This is a trend among younger people. Pro-GameStop investors believed that GameStop could transform its stores, reduce clutter and transform them into sleek immersive hubs in which gamers can congregate and enjoy gaming on a completely new dimension. GameStop is the perfect place to do this. There is already space available for it; the cost will be minimal and it will yield huge dividends with the growth of online gaming or professional-grade gaming events. There's a market for gaming events that allow gamers to meet and lose themselves for hours of immersive gaming experiences , while also having the option of purchasing games, such as Dungeons & Dragons gamers small tournaments, showcases and more. Professional gamers and other gamers might even entertain a crowd in the same space (Preston 2020).

GameStop may also collaborate with other vendors such as Electronic Arts and Activision to bring new games to its stores, and offer exclusive test-before-you-buy opportunities as they have evolved into more than just a place that you can buy items. Professional gamers could collaborate with brands to organize events in conjunction with these launches. A fresh and modernized GameStop could be a viable option and they've already tested the new configuration at Tulsa, Oklahoma, and it was a huge success with plans to expand it to other locations (Preston 2020).

With these thoughts in mind, perhaps GameStop could become an Starbucks to gamers. However, can they be able to do it in a timely manner and with enough intelligence, and will it be profitable over time? It is contingent on a number of things happening right and leveraging the possibilities offered by the latest console cycle as well as the variety of games that accompany it. This could provide them with a swift cash boost that will help them move their business towards the most profitable route.

Analysts such as Scott Preston thought, by 2022 it would be too to be late and everything would be in decline from that point on. Thus, GameStop needed that cash injection to move quickly and profit from the opportunities and assets that could arise.

If it can actually be done or even go as planned is in doubt. Certain institutional investors didn't believe that. This belief could have been more severe in the course of the epidemic, when the cost of GameStop shares slowly increased as smaller investors started to buy into the company's stock.

New Management and a New Direction

The year 2020 was the time that GameStop revealed its management change after the team attempted diversifying their business and other strategies which didn't work well. The new team was able to refocus because, after these unsuccessful changes they understood their customers more (Preston 2020). This was a good sign of a shift.

The new management is similar to the new head coach for an athletic team that is not performing well because the former coach, despite being good in past times, screwed things up. This gives fans lots of confidence when they are confident their new manager is experienced and knows what they're doing. Similar to this with businesses. Like any sports enthusiast will inform that the new coach isn't the answer to every team's issues However, they are crucial to the success of the team. They can aid in restructuring the team, find the best talent and implement the most effective strategies. In some instances the head coach, regardless of how skilled they are, is not able to save an entire team when the structures that are that are in place aren't sufficient or there aren't enough resources available. It's a difficult task. From the viewpoint as a short seller, this was the case at GameStop The new employees weren't ready for the job or they were fighting an uphill struggle, which it certainly was.

Gamestop Only has one move

Citron Research has said the only thing that could justify the GameStop price is if they acquired Esports Entertainment Group, an online company that offers esports betting (Weil 2021, 2021). This is how GameStop could make money from its massive customer database. Citron Research thinks if it decides to do this the price of its shares could go at least $50. This is a claim that was that was made earlier this year, following the frenzied events of last year. However, in the typical short-seller way, we do not know the exact reasons they used for short-selling GameStop.

*

Arguments similar to those presented above succeeded in persuading a lot of investors who were small of the need to buy GameStop, regardless of the arguments they could be presented with. The rise of social media as well as the convenience trading platforms such as Robinhood brought everything to the point of boiling. The shift was triggered in the early part of February 2020 and at the close of the year the cost for GameStop shares had increased by between $18 and $4.

What's At Stake?

If the GameStop customers were correct, they would have created one of the most profitable investments of their lives. The money they made could increase by a lot. This is exactly the goal they had in mind.

In addition, they can create enthusiasm and interest to an organization that is on its last phase and provide it with an opportunity to re-enter the market, which could be required to pivot and stay alive. If stocks are only speculated between buyers and sellers what happens? If there's enough interest in stocks and companies, it could issue additional shares to fund itself since there is a demand for these shares. Media coverage can turn the public's opinion around and the public could wish for the company to be successful and will support it with an active effort. The current environment of social media has enabled people to work in highly coordinated ways, and more than they ever have before. Strange things can happen and what starts out as an ordinary short-squeeze or pump-and-dump operation could result in doing a great deal of good, including saving as well as creating employment. As with many things that damage the Internet generally, we don't realize until it's already taking place.

It may seem evident, but it's important to note that short sellers themselves are wrong , and they've often been incorrect. There is nothing definitively true regarding the arguments they make. In the end, at all times, individuals can and do mimic companies' successes when they cooperate.

Chapter 8: The Squeeze

It was impossible to predict how the pandemic in the world will impact the economy. GameStop was to be expected to get huge cash in 2020 due to the release of new gaming consoles and games. However, the releases were ultimately delayed , and then later delayed. The overall economy was not doing well. Many people were unemployed and for those with jobs, their wages were dropping because of the election. The dramas surrounding it took the center stage. Republicans as well as Democrats were at war over a crucial second stimulus bill. Families faced evictions and lots of people were dying. The situation was chaotic and tragic.

I bring these points up because they are a hostile environment for businesses to operate in. Companies require people who have funds to spend. They require people to work; they require people to perform. If they're not getting those things done it means there's less money in the economy, which generally results in a decrease in sales. Most of the money accessible is used for essential products and services.

It is understandable that you wouldn't think of a business like GameStop to be successful in this market. Perhaps in the case of an IT business or a vital product or service provider and it would. However, when the buying and the working habits of a lot of customers moved to online shopping the company was able to highlight the aspect that GameStop wasn't skilled in.

On the 8th of December, 2020, Xbox made a statement it's net revenue were down by 30% during the third quarter. However its online sales were up by over 250%. Furthermore, it was predicted that it would do much better during the 4th quarter since it was the time for the Xbox X series and PlayStation 5 were just launched in November (Gamestop Corporation. 2020). When a company makes use of numbers like this they are used to create a positive impression even though 250% sounds like a good number however, it could mean nothing in actual numbers, such as an increase of 1000 users up to 3500. The reason they didn't reveal the number of customers who visited the online store been a red flag to an intelligent investor. However, the performance of the company was not particularly good and its shares fell from $13 to $13.

The company was aware that it could be in danger, and they believed that a management change could be a catalyst to turn things up in the right direction by appointing Alan Attal, Ryan Cohen as well as Jim Grube. Cohen was known for establishing and directing Chewy the online eCommerce site that sells pet-related items. Attal was chief marketing officer at Chewy. Gruber is the head of finance of Chewy (Thorbecke 2021). Together, they worked to build the company into the point it is now and a huge success. They seemed to be the perfect combination to help GameStop successfully move into a new phase.

On paper, this selection is a good one. They put together an all-star team who previously worked together. There was already a relationship between them and the goal was to entice a large number of GameStop fans. In the wake of that confirmation, there was some excitement within WallStreetBets. This was a positive signal. The following day, the price increased to $22. The next day the price of the stock jumped to $31.40.

Keith Gill couldn't believe it. He'd been working to promote GameStop for months. And it appeared as if his investments were yielding results. He made a return investment in the early days when the stock was four dollars or less. After the press release was released He shared images of his investment on the WallStreetBets subreddit, which generated a lot of discussions and announcements. It's easy to imagine how exciting this could have been. The shift in leadership was thrilling enough. Add your own who was making money on a plan they'd developed for some time, and it appeared that it was going to benefit others. The stock was inexpensive and they could easily get in should they want. Why shouldn't they?

In the years that followed it was believed that the company was of worth and could be redeemed strongly shook the minds of traders who were small. Michael Burry M.D as portrayed in the movie The Big Short, was the main reason for this notion because he believed in the same idea (Thorbecke 2021) and made the idea of investing in the company more attractive. There was probably an anxiety about not having fun with the WallStreetBets community (though it was not at the heights it was likely to eventually reach). In the end, a significant portion from the WallStreetBets community started to buy GameStop.

In the meantime, there also were Melvin Capital and Citron Capital. There were probably other companies that decided to sell short GameStop however the biggest and most infamous of them were Melvin Capital and Citron Capital. It's hard to pinpoint what time the two firms took on position in the short market, however we do know that they did.

As the world became aware of the scandal and found out the major perpetrators this made the investing even more thrilling, especially if it was with Andrew Left. As we've seen, Left is not the most pleasant voice on Wall Street, well known for his short-term stance on companies prior to publishing and spreading negative things about them. Even if he's right his short-selling smears might be difficult to accept.

On the 18th of January in 2021 Left's Citron Research was able to do something that only stirred the flames: They began targeting small investors who jumped onto GameStop.

Here's how it got began:

Tomorrow at 11:11 Eastern Standard Time Citron will stream live five reasons GameStop players who purchase $GME with these prices are winners in this poker game. The stock is back to $20 in a short time. We are more knowledgeable about short interest than you do, and we will tell you why.

Thanks to viewers for their feedback on the last streamed tweet.-Citron research (2021)

Here's how it were accepted:

There was a mistake with NIO, Palantir, Tesla, Plug Power & Shopify. These companies are here for the purpose of manipulating markets to earn a quick profit. Don't fall for their trap of bois. They only want to make gains.--Bryant (2021)

You guys have a close 100% coin flip accuracy rate. You're no better then us.--Sentinnel (2021)

The answer from small traders is hilarious since-as the case with these kinds of things--it's true. They cite the instances when Citron Research has failed at prediction of stock prices, and then quote their low success rate.

The video Citron Research posted is now removed from YouTube however, they did livestream in which they outlined their case. On the 21stof the month, the price of the stock had risen to $40. If there's something we've learned about the Internet it is that you shouldn't take a joke or try to mock your rivals particularly when they're an entire mob and you're only one man.

The following day when the cost of GameStop was not down by $20 but was up by $25 ending at $65. It could have been a bit of a warning signal to the suits on Wall Streets, but perhaps it appeared that the market was going to end up being a flop and prices would go back to their previous levels. The support for WallStreetBets was growing however, there was a sense of excitement throughout the air. The victory was streamed in real-time on the channel of Gill through the YouTube channel.

On the 25th of March day of the month, the stock traded at $96. The price reached a peak of $159. The suits may have been concerned however, the price was reduced to $76 at the close. It was beginning to look like it was fast-running out and everything would unfold like they were predicted. The price wouldn't plunge into the floor, however it appeared as if the floor was about to be able to cave in.

Then,something that no one could ever account for happened: Elon Musk tweeted one word--"GameStonk!"--and a link to the WallStreetBets subreddit (Thorbecke, 2021).

Elon Musk was well-known on the subreddit and, at the time of his tweet, he had more than 44 million people following him on Twitter. That's a lot to influence in the culture that is dominated by people who worship and praise wealthy and successful individuals. It was unclear what the message meant, however the message was received well by the subreddit and they felt that they were supported. It appeared that he was on the position of the smaller investors, and perhaps even putting his money into the market. Another thing that the suits did not anticipate was that a renowned venture capitalist, Chamath Palaihapitiya who tweeted that he'd like to be investing in GameStop (Thorbecke 2021). What further proof would you require to be sure you're not in doubt? The story morphed from a minor squabble to the forefront of a bold initiative.

The night before, the buzz of activities on WallStreetBets was awe-inspiring with memes galore as well as "Let's bring GameStop up to the sky!" trending. It was exciting, energetic and fun.

To better understand the hype, keep in mind that for those first four days prior to the Elon Musk tweets GameStop is referred to as being a stock with a viral appeal that was the focus of an online mob who would go to any lengths to prop up the price in order to show their point, and journalists sat in awe.

But it is important to be aware that there could be a romantic aspect of the purchase. It is logical that investors would invest all their energy and enthusiasm in something that they feel at least a little bit enthusiastic about. I'm certain that a large portion of the members on subreddit were able to recall positive experiences with GameStop and some might have even employed there.

It's worth explaining the short squeeze. The reason a firm shorts its stock is that they need to offer collateral, including the cost, as the case if you were making loans. This will give the owner of the stock some assurance that you are willing to repay. It can also allow them to make more money from their shares. Collateral is based on the risk as well as the amount of shares in question. When the risks are large it is necessary to have more collateral and so on. What happens when the value of the stock increases is that collateral becomes needed.

Take it from the point of view of a person who has just given an hedge fund shares and watched the value of the stock increase. They are worried because they consider, "Okay, they might never be capable of paying me back." This is why they request more security in order to be sure they are compensated should the company fail to pay back their stock. I'm sure you'd like to take the same approach should you be in the same position.

Additionally this means that the company is required to purchase the stock at a greater price. This purchase will boost the price since it is a naturally aggressive. When these two forces clash and buyers take the price up and additional collateral required and the investment company feeling under pressure because they are ordered to pay for both sides. There is only one way to stop the situation is to purchase the stock back and then returning it regardless of price. Be aware that there's the possibility that the person who owns the stock could ask the company to exchange their shares back. in that case the company has to purchase the stock immediately. This is not a good thing for the business as they must close the position sooner than they would have thought of. This is a problem because it's against the idea of a company waiting for a while to reap the rewards. In the end, the momentum will diminish and they'll be able to sell the shares at a cheaper cost.

However, if the buyer is not willing to compromise or is no longer interested, the company must take back the stock at the rate it's being sold at. It is clear that the short squeeze can create an opportunity that's not an easy one for a business to get out of, particularly when buyers are highly motivated and determined. This is in the event that buyers realize what they're doing and really are determined to cause harm. This is exactly what we started witnessing.

WallStreetBets enjoyed a great deal of joy in doing this since they did really dislike Andrew Left, his condescending tone and the Wall Street kin. There are also allegations that WallStreetBets Redditors have hacked Citron Research Twitter (Thorbecke 2021) and YouTube (McGrath 2021). The allegations stem direct to Citron Research, and they aren't confirmed yet however, it's reasonable to believe that something similar could be the case, as it's not unreasonable to consider certain members of WallStreetBets as the smartest and most sophisticated individuals. If they could be in a position to make profits from memes an organization, they would definitely be able to do more.

These four days, which ran from 22nd to 26th, resulted in something astonishing that was a clash that took many forms between two titans that were wildly opposed of the financial market. Experts were saying something, but the smaller investors were saying something different. The experience of Wall Street shows it tends to be a single-minded sway However, the trending topics on social media suggested there was something more to it.

The argument that was centered around an organization turned into something completely different which is where I believe the concern really began. There was some concern over the weekend, but it could have been minimal perhaps Andrew Left got emails and calls from clients. they worked to get things under control because at this point, there was nothing to worry about. It's easy to think of how the calls could have been: "It's just a bunch of kids using trading apps. They're not sure how they're acting. They're just making fun. This will go away similar to the typical Twitter trend in an hour or so. There is not something to be concerned about."

If there an expert in social media close to him, they may have shared with him megatrends. Megatrends are when something that is posted is trending on social media globally. Megatrends can be compared to those problems that your boss pushed you to take on, such as those of the Ice Bucket Challenge or Mannequin Challenge which is why they upload it to the corporate social media page using the appropriate hashtag to keep it relevant.

Everybody takes on the task. The funny thing concerning GameStop is that the exact kind of thing took place. If something is successful enough, everyone is eager to be a part of it. And everybody is eager to take part in it.

Certain people have been rightly critical of tweets by Elon Musk and some investors to increase the excitement. This has been a source of accusations of market manipulation. If those accusations are true, it is not the main point of this debate. Only one thing can keep this war from happening is to capitulate early. The game would be over because there's no conflict between the suits and the minor guys. The rise of social media and the increasing trend of financial markets has created markets that are more vulnerable to all sorts of distortions and manipulations. It is because of the way that flamboyant and contagious social media is. Certain Wall Street players are very aware of this and I'm sure that some were able to profit from the opportunity they bought into and chose to side with the small players. Maybe they were wise enough to be able to tell when to go out or enter the market. It is believed that not recognizing the impact of social media in affecting the market for stocks is what caused the next event.

On the 26th of May, Citron Research announced they were closing their positions. Andrew Left famously said,"This has attracted the interest of America and all traders as well as trader and non-trader" (Thorbecke 2021).

It's a crucial quote to mention because as soon as the man said that it was evident that the company was in serious problems. When more customers are piled on, this could increase prices which is exactly what was the case.

The cost of GameStop was so high that it reached the moon. Remember those rocket emojis? The stock reopened the following day at $354.00 and the major investment firms were forced to sell their shares with a huge loss. It's believed the company Melvin Capital lost about 53 percent of its investments. The company had entered the year with around $12 billion. They left in January with just $8 billion after receiving bailouts of more than $2.5 billion by Citadel (Goodwin 2021).

Left then told BBC that he received an increase of around 20%, however Left would not reveal the exact amount he actually lost. Similar is the case about Melvin Capital because it's only published by The Wall Street Journal that they lost the same amount, but the exact figures aren't disclosed. There's a evidence to suggest that the disparity between the two numbers could be due to Melvin Capital stuck on a bit longer as Citron Capital. Or, was in a higher short-term loan, which is why it suffered more losses and needed an emergency bailout.

However, the mood that day was electric; the narrative that was told was one of Redditors facing Wall Street, a story of David and Goliath and of Reddit Kraken slayers taking on Wall Street giants. There was plenty of excitement and excitement on the internet. the internet was abuzz with this tale. Every aspect of our media was affected. What happened was that people who had not thought of trading or investing put their money in GameStop because that's what everyone else was doing and they were making a mess of Wall Street.

It wasn't just the tales of the guys posting on Reddit now. For instance in the New York Times told stories of high school students who could earn thousands, ten-year olds making money (Morales 2021) as well as an ordained pastor and his wife who said: "There's a catharsis to earning money from their suffering a bit. Take the rich" (Phillips and Lorenz 2021).

An account such as "just received Robinhood and made this incredible investment, and earned some money" is a powerful and inspirational story to share. The message was fairly consistent: They didn't mind whether they made or lost money, they simply wanted to get the big guys get hurt.

As stated in the article by Bloomberg columnist Matt Levine, the amount the hedge funds suffered was not that large (2021). It wasn't enough to cause them to fail. them, but on social media there was a different story. It's not a secret that they suffered injuries, but the amount they suffered was just exaggerated like so often happens in the world of Internet.

It was a huge victory for the small guy -- more about this in the future. However, at the conclusion of the day the dragon wasn't defeated and no krakens given in to the power of the mass. There was no Wall Street revolution taking place but the seismic risk factor was added. It's not a detract of the fact that it was an enormous success. It's something that's not happened before. I cannot stress this enough. This is one of the situations you'd never imagine would occur.

We must be attentive to what transpired the following day. The rapid increase that was GameStop continued. The stock reached an all-time high of $483 but it then closed at $193.00. What transpired was that Robinhood prevented its customers from purchasing GameStop and restricted selling. Other stocks affected included AMC and Nokia that had been targeted by the WallStreetBets campaign. It was a way for the price of Nokia to fall. In some cases,

Robinhood closed some of its customers' positions without their consent. This led to a lot of debate.

The result was the well-known Chris Cuomo interview where the chief executive of Robinhood, Vlad Tenev, was asked questions about the matter. Cuomo began the interview by saying "I would like you to acknowledge the obvious. It appears to be a move from an application known as Robinhood which claims to take money from the rich and give it to the less fortunate however, it is doing the opposite. When the big players including one of the major investors of your company began to lose it was time to end the game in order to feed the poor" (CNN 2021).

Robinhood claimed that this wasn't what was going on. The general impression was "Of Of course Robinhood will deny it. They wouldn't admit it , as it would hurt their image. We know for a fact that this is exactly what they did."

The Twitter community as well as many others were searching for alternatives to purchase GameStop and to get rid of the infamous Robinhood. There was an outpouring of anger at Robinhood and Tenev was not able to do a great job in calming the masses. The questionable nature of his business model exposed through Chris Cuomo went down as one of the main reasons to fight for the poor people.

However, were these allegations truthful or fair? We'll get to the issue in the near future. The most important thing to take away from this incident is the way it was presented to the general public. The story was told that we heard, and we watched many politicians like Representative Alexandria Ocasio-Cortez and others, respond in a very strong way to this. Ocasio-Cortez tweeted (2021):

This is inadmissible.

We are now required to learn more about

The discussion then turned to manipulating markets, which is a word that was being frequently used that it was compared to profanity. This is due to it being known that Citadel the company that saved Melvin

Capital, was also a major customer of Robinhood. Because they pay for orders flow, which is the reason why in March Elizabeth Warren tweeted (2021):

Robinhood was hit with a class-action suit due to the decision and the demise of GameStop. The stock would rise once more after Robinhood permitted customers to purchase. GameStop's price would hit $415 before closing at $350.00.

The discussion was lively within the WallStreetBets community on the next steps to take Do they want to hold or buy more shares? Is it the right the time to sell?

As of this time, all the major hedge funds had already taken out. Melvin Capital and Citron Capital had closed its positions by the 27th January. The flurry of activity that took place after the day seemed unmotivated. You can't cause harm to the big boys even if they weren't. However, there were reports that hedge funds were in short positions and had conspired in conjunction with media outlets to claim they were closing their positions. This is more difficult to prove and more difficult to believe, but there were those who believed. It's not an absurd notion to believe, as corporations are adept at spouting stories.

In response to a question to comment, Professor and economist RichardD. Wolff provided this information regarding GameStop and the market for stocks: "If you pump information through the Internet nowadays-through newspapers as well as radio from the past, you can make people take action. You then bet on what they'll be doing. Then, you realize that the stock market is all about. It's about the gamblers who bet on the likelihood that they have tricked the public by carefully arranging information of one type or other." Wolff added,, "We don't know what's going on inside a company. We let corporations provide us details, and newspaper reports reiterate about what's happening. However, if you've ever worked in a business. You're aware that there's something called 'creative accounting. What you write, even on the form you give for the public, could be easily misrepresented, just as it is, actually, truthful. There is a lot of reasons to be dishonest" (The Hill 2021).

This is because these incidents including hedge funds cutting their positions, took place prior to Robinhood's decision indicates that the argument that was being made about Robinhood protecting large investors was a lie. It could mean something far worse than a shady eating-the-rich story. Many people were enticed to invest with this false narrative and they lost lots of money.

The message being circulated, via memes and all caps as well as using rocket emojis, included "hold." The message was followed by some discussion on the next step when they decide to either sell or hold, however most of the messages were the second. Investors who were smarter were selling when the price was very high. They required others to hold to make sure that prices didn't drop dramatically. They made lots of cash. Remember that each time someone earns money from markets, somebody is unable to make it back, and those individuals are usually the least knowledgeable and unaware of the circumstance they're in. This is true for small investors as well as the general public.

The reality is that the value of the stock will fall and people who have stock prices go down are likely to end up having less money than they used to have, and lose everything, or be stuck with useless stocks. There were people who lost money. Most people were attracted by the spectacle, not really thinking about what was happening. Why do I talk all the time about this? It's because it's an empty and pump, an opposite to the short and distort. The techniques are similar.

In his piece Pumps and Chumps and Dumps Nobel-prize-winning economist Paul Krugman explains: "A pump and dump happens whenever an investment firm or a group of investors purchase shares inexpensively and then force its price higher by propagating misinformation or rumors and then letting them dump their shares to naive chumps, or bag holders' at an profit. It's a logical and illegal act, however it's highly unlikely that anyone will be prosecuted in the GameStop scandal since it'll likely be difficult to establish the intent.

The shares did, in actual become pumped. We don't even know who specifically pushed GameStop However, many WallStreetBets posts are reported to be being generated by bots, not real humans. And someone made a fortune by selling the stock to bags owners" (2021).

Is this a false-information campaign? Maybe. Who were the people who were chumps? The general population and possibly large portions from the WallStreetBets community.

Let's begin with the obvious.

Claim One Hedge Funds and Citadel Blocked Trading to protect themselves

It's not the case. Citadel is Robinhoods market maker, this means that they gain from the fact that more traders are executed regardless of what the trades. In the past, we discussed the way market makers operate. Although Citadel might have an influence on Robinhood in this manner but it's still not enough to explain the reason other trading platforms temporarily suspended meme stocks such as GameStop.

The reason for this is that clearinghouses. When you buy shares on Robinhood, Robinhood goes to the stock exchange, or any other place they can find the quantity of shares you'd like for the price you quoted. Then, an agreement is made by you with the vendor. However, shares can take up to three days to move between one individual to the next or to be finalized. This is the same as owning real estate. If you're a purchaser seeking a security that you will receive the shares that are registered in your name. If you sell and want to be sure that you'll get your money. Clearinghouses guarantee you that your transfer is going to take place through the act of an intermediary between the seller and buyer and selling to the buyer. The only thing they require as collateral. This collateral is known as the margin. It is a percentage of the worth of the transaction. this money will be returned once the transfer is completed. Instead of putting your faith in a person you've never had the pleasure of meeting, all you're dealing with is a reputable institution that will issue your shares. It's the same with the seller. When you purchase shares the broker will put up collateral in the shape of an investment. The more risky and volatile the deal is, the greater the deposit that your broker needs to make. It is clear the direction I'm going in this.

If a large number of people are purchasing stocks in high quantities as well as frequency, then they will need to provide more collateral. This means they might be short of cash and be in a position to finance other elements of their business, particularly when the particular stock is highly risky.

This is why Vlad Tenev, CEO of Robinhood was forced to block the purchase of GameStop. They didn't have the funds. That's the reason they were forced to wait either to obtain more finance or for deals to be concluded and for the funds to be returned. The details of how this process works aren't easy to understand however, this is how it is done in a concise manner.

This is also the reason the reason Robinhood has sold certain shares of its customers in order that they could lessen the pressure they were feeling. Tenev might have claimed they didn't had problems with liquidity, but that is exactly what they did and that's what Tenev said. A business that claims it is dealing with a liquidity issue is not appealing to investors, and there's no reason to acknowledge that they have a liquidity issue unless the situation is so serious that they could be accused of negligence if they don't.

This is the second aspect: There's an enormous attraction for an investor such as Citadel to fulfill orders since this is how they earn their money. The money they would have earned from a situation such a scenario is far more than the return on the Melvin Capital investment. It is not logical for companies to refuse investment opportunities; it is the main reason they exist.

However, does being rescued by an industry maker gives you an advantage? It certainly is. There's probably some sort of advantage from knowing which deals are being signed and the frequency at which they're being done. The legality of this , or the details of what's happening is a different subject completely.

Second Claim: The Short-Sellers Lose $70 Billion, and Bankrupted Them

This is a false representation of the Reuters report that states the total loss from trading in short positions in market prices in the United States is $70 billion to date (Rao 2021) . This is not in connection with GameStop. Hedge funds lost approximately $1 billion on short positions in relation to GameStop and the short position studied in the data comprised over 5,000 investments companies (Rao 2021).

As we've already seen that the hedge funds didn't fail to go into bankruptcy. They did lose a significant amount of their capital but not all of it.

So, What Did Happen Next?

On day, GameStop began trading at $379, and closed at $325 following reaching as high as $413. It was showing early signs of decline exactly as it was forecasted. But, a major indicator of significance for WallStreetBets came with the declaration made by Andrew Left that he would not publish any more short reports--you know, the reports that he had been writing about companies he was shorting to ensure the value of their stock would fall. If there's something that is certain during this entire process something is that things have changed for Wall Street, it is the realization that WallStreetBets as well as social media platforms can use and inspire reports like this to create chaos.

There are some who are hired only to monitor the WallStreetBets who are on call to inform their employers of developments and threats before they occur. They might even be able to influence trends or even the tone of the forum. This is certainly a difficult task however it's not difficult. The institutions they work with are able to access a lot of resources and have the ability to hire the best individuals, including trading influencers who don't elude the lure of cash. The Goliath of Wall Street always finds a way, it's their game and they're the ones who play it.

Furthermore it is a fact Reddit is so well-known and anonymous could easily be used to gain access and be compromised, which exposes it to manipulation. We've seen this. We discussed earlier whom was responsible for the squeeze since it seems like some one was behind it. This is attributable to the character of Reddit. It's susceptible to such manipulations.

The following Monday GameStop stocks continued to fall. They started at $360, climbed as high as $322 and ended at $225. The next day, the same occurred: GameStop opened at $140 but then went up to $156, before closing at $90.00. It's almost like watching the drama unfold, when investors, both regular and redditors tried to maintain the price however the price declined every day. The price opens, and then goes up slightly, but then it plummets dramatically. The close of the week, GameStop was selling for $63. The 19th of February the stock was worth $40. The crash was over, but was that the end?

It is not certain that any of this could result in regulation or change in the way the market functions However, it was likely an key questions that were asked during the hearings to be held in Congress.

Chapter 9: Technicalities

One of the less understood aspects is how the men from WallStreetBets caused the stock price to go up. A lot of people believe that they bought the stock for themselves, which is not true at all. To fully understand what they bought it is necessary to examine what we call options.

Options are contracts in which the underlying value depends on the value of another investment, like stocks. To understand the purpose of options it is important to comprehend options as betting on the price of the stock will rise or fall. For instance, if, for example, you wager that the price of a certain stock will be greater than $10 and you prove correct, you are granted the option to purchase the stock for $10 regardless of whether the current stock cost is more. The price you purchase this stock for is known as"the strike price. For this bet you pay only a fee which is in essence an expense or cost of the bet.

On the other side of this agreement is another person who will offer you shares at the price you choose if you are right. If you're not and they take the money you have put down to bet. This is where the notion that it's an agreement comes from. In essence, all bets, including those in casinos, are contract between yourself and someone who puts into a bet with you.

There are two kinds of bets. One is a bet on the possibility that price increase that is known as an option to call or a bet that the price will fall that is known as"put. In addition to placing bets, but you could also play the role of a bookmaker. You can offer option options, or even call options. If you sell them you're hoping that the person who purchases your option isn't a fool. Options come with expiry dates and they may expire as either worthless or valuable. If a call option expires worthless simply means that your prediction was not correct, or you wouldn't have earned profits if you had decided to exercise your option. Each option is comprised of 100 shares as its base asset. Let's look at a few examples.

Let's say you purchase an option to call with the strike price of $20 for $5. This means that you've placed an bet of $500 on the possibility that your stock would have a value of at least $20 prior to the expiration date. If the price of this stock increases to $28 prior to when the contract expires, you'll be able to purchase 100 shares at $28, even though they are currently selling for $28. This means you will get $3 less per share (remember that you placed a bet of $5 per share in order to bet). If you wish to sell the shares immediately, you can sell the shares for $28 and take the $3 profit you earned by selling the shares. This means that you'll earn around $300 in profit following the first investment of 500 dollars. This is a profit of 60%.

Options on stocks are less expensive when compared to normal stocks, but the risk involved in investing in stock options is greater. If you're not right about the bet you placed, you'll will lose everything. If you purchase stocks, even if the price does not rise then you still own the stock. You could sell it to get the money back, or keep it until the price increases and then decide to sell.

What usually happens is that when a person purchases an option to call, which is a wager that the stock will rise and that the person selling the option to them will have to purchase a part of the stock even if they don't have it. This serves as a means to limit their risk and the amount they pay for will be different based on the risks involved.

If I purchase the Tesla call option that has the strike price of $400, and I'm hoping that the price will go upwards to around $430, the person selling will need to enter the market and purchase Tesla shares while it's still below the current price of its stock.

They aren't buying too many shares--about 10 percent of the contract is likely to be bought to ensure that they don't lose a large amount of money if they're incorrect. They also alter the number of shares they buy when the value of the stock fluctuates. This helps to prevent purchasing the stock at a very high price only to sell them to me at a cheaper price, and making money. This is a preemptive measure and also preventive.

Buy as many call options as you can will increase prices due to the fact that call writers, who are market makers in the majority of instances need to travel out and purchase that stock to reduce risks. If they are doing this in a hurry they cause the price of the stock rise. This can trigger an unintended chain reaction where market makers who are managing their risks increase prices as people decide to decide to exercise their call options because prices went up and on and on. This is exactly what happened in this WallStreetBets and GameStop story. The reason for this was the stock market and an unprecedented flood of call options that were aggressive that drove prices up.

Naturally, once the less-experienced traders were able to join in the height of the mania they were unable to comprehend the subtleties of what was happening which led to them purchasing the stock in whole instead of leveraging some their positions by leveraging options on stock or any different financial instruments.

Jaime Rogozinski has observed a stark link between the increase in the number of WallStreetBets membership and launch of options for stocks on platforms such as Robinhood (2020) .

It is a good thing since stock options are inexpensive and buying stocks directly is costly. It is generally an excellent option. There's always the possibility that the price will rise because of an unexpected event and you could at the very least get some of your investment back. However, stock options can be profitable at just a tiny amount. In addition, they don't have to pay commissions on the profits. This makes them appealing to those who prefer trading apps with no commissions.

It's well-documented within the world of finance that younger generations are especially cautious because they don't have to worry about retirement , or paying for mortgages and other obligations. They are able to take risks earlier since they've got the space to recuperate.

If we continue to assume that there are people who would like to take advantage of the community, it makes sense. These groups could have an in-depth knowledge of the psychology of the population.

However, I'm moving closer to more conspiracist views and I'm not looking to be a part of this. It's interesting to contemplate.

The increase in stock trading interest isn't just due to commission-free or low commission applications. It's also due to investment instruments which are generally speaking, low-cost.

Therefore, it's not a stretch to imagine that these customers especially in WallStreetBets were playing with extremely complicated financial instruments that they were knowledgeable in complex financial situations better than ordinary people even if they lost funds.

Short squeezes and how they executed it demonstrate this. The team saw an opening and they seized the opportunity, and it was impressive due to all the other aspects that are involved in the way markets function.

Let's take an example: You bet that GameStop will be $20 within a week. At the moment, GameStop is trading at $12.00. To place a bet it's going to cost $5. Then, multiply that number by 100, which means that placing the bet will cost you $500.

If after a week you're right when the cost of GameStop increases to $30, that gives you the chance to buy 100 shares for $20 each however, the price for GameStop is currently for thirty dollars per share. Instead of paying $3000 to buy 100 shares, you'll end up paying $2,000, which means you only paid $500 to place that bet. However, if you're proved incorrect, you've lost $500 completely.

If you're in the end but do not have enough money to buy the shares for $2,000, then you could always take out a loan or sell your winning stock to someone who is willing to purchase the stock at a discounted price. The majority of people take funds from brokers.

It is also possible to use options as a form of insurance. As an example, suppose you own 100 shares of GameStop and GameStop is highly volatile; you could earn profit when GameStop is up and down and it drops. You can purchase put options that allow you to sell the stock at a price that is higher than its market value in the event that the stock price declines. You can then purchase it again at a cheaper price and make profits. If you purchase put options then you are betting that the value for the shares will decrease.

A lot of people in the WallStreetBets community earned money during the week they were there because they didn't have to be able to pay for the stock, they simply required the ability to make use of stock options.

Chapter 10: Hearings

On February 18 The House Committee on Financial Services conducted a hearing on the GameStop incident that took place. The primary focus of the hearing was to determine whether there was any improper actions on both parties. There was no clear reason for what the purpose of the hearing was. Many journalists have described it as theatre because it's unlikely to produce anything significant out of the hearing. There's a bit of truth to the accusations.

It's fascinating that, regardless of this criticism certain of the issues that were raised in the hearing were crucial to knowing what happened and the significance. The entire incident had revealed gaps and weaknesses in the system and the hearing was a great way of highlighting these. That's not saying that without the hearing there wouldn't be plenty of discussion in the pages of Bloomberg forums, forums, and blogs to shed spotlight on these issues, however, a hearing is more entertaining, which is the theater component of the process.

The witnesses who attended the hearing included Keith Gill, Kenneth Griffin of Citadel, Vlad Tenev of Robinhood and Steve Huffman from Reddit. Huffman was not as prominent as the other participants; he was more similar to the furnishings in the room, but not the center of the spotlight. Gill, Griffin, and Tenev were the main focus. This is why we were all watching.

I will discuss some of the most important questions that were asked during the hearing as well as what the answers were.

Are Robinhood Customers Getting the Best Deal?

One question put to the panelists was the question of whether Robinhood users are given less favorable treatment due to the fact that they don't have to pay commissions in any way. Robinhood's business relies heavily on the market maker more than its customers. Users on Robinhood's platform are more similar to capitalists than customers. This raises the question What is the best way to determine if Robinhood prioritize the demands of its users over its large market maker customers? Since users of Robinhood don't have to pay commissions, they may not be receiving the right treatment. Therefore, when market makers receive an order, there's a reason to believe they may take orders from Robinhood in a less favorable manner as compared to orders from premium brokers.

This question was addressed at Griffin of Citadel who could not provide a definitive answer. He was unable to come up with a solution because the person asking the question did not intend to accommodate any kind of nuance, so he demanded the answer to be a yes or no. What happens behind the scenes of these transactions is extremely complex and calls for more complex explanations, however that doesn't necessarily mean that a simple yes or no answer is impossible. However, CEOs like Griffin do not like to answer this question because it can make them look bad.

There are plenty of good reasons to think that Robinhood customers aren't receiving the most value for money. It's true that you pay what you spend for you know?

Hedging Funds as well as Market Manipulation

Another topic of discussion is whether hedge funds or banks were involved in manipulating markets when it came to shorting GameStop. This is due to the fact that GameStop had a short-interest that was around 140%, which means that the shorts were shortened by investors more than GameStop did. This kind of aggressive approach could result in prices falling below what is reasonable, which seems crazy when you consider it. This means that some investors were selling shares they hadn't taken out, referred to in the industry as "empty" shares. This isn't legally permitted. There are a lot of concerns about the way that this occurred: Who was the person responsible and who paid for the transaction?

The practice of shorting more shares than a company is allowed to short artificially pushes the price of the stock down. This, in an aspect, is a form of manipulating markets.

Short sellers might have valid argument to think that a company's value is too high however this is suspicious. That's one of the reasons that angered small investors. They considered themselves to be being in the same boat as the rest of us Robinhood's actions seemed to be a deliberate one.

Short selling by distorting effects is just like the pump and dump at the end of the day. It's an extremely effective method of transferring funds from the weaker to the more powerful. But, as with every Wall Street steal, there is always a chance.

There's no reason to doubt that other investors were looking at GameStop and thought that the value of its stock was insane. In a way the price was actually due to the fact that it was artificially adjusted due to a massively unsettling short-term interest.

This question didn't get any straight answer.

Robinhood's Blocking Decision

If Robinhood has hurt its customers through its decision to restrict the purchase of certain stocks was a query that required an answer, if it was not due to the interest the decision received. The answer is yes, it did. If people were unable to buy stocks and selling was one of the options, prices fell, and those who were hoping that prices would increase were unable to make a profit. That's the primary reason why lots of people were upset.

Representative Alexandria Ocasio Cortez further pondered this issue , asking whether Robinhood should channel some of the funds by the flow of payments and distribute it to customers who have lost money due to the decision they made. Robinhood was in self-preservation mode to the detriment of its customers. However, it is possible to argue that having done so could have been much more detrimental for a larger number of consumers (CNBC Television 2021).

Tenev was not keen on being asked these kinds of questions. It was evident that the man didn't wish to. The reasons I've given ought to explain the reasons he didn't wish to. He helped the company out with the help of a few users , and could have avoided the greater damage.

It could have been effective for Robinhood but the fact that they had to stop buying for a set period of time it also pushed GameStop to go popular, and a lot more people joined in more than they had before. So, more cash was taken out of fingers of those who were vulnerable.

I understand that this was a choice they had to take in order to protect the business they had built, however it is not to be denied how devastating this decision was to a lot of people. Robinhood is currently being sued in more than 90 lawsuits as a result of this event. The level of pain that people feel is what makes this hearing an event that was a blockbuster.

It's essential in a sense, since it is important to be able to sense as if things are being done and that the authorities take this very seriously. There's a sense of catharsis. Political leaders must be on the side of the people and citizens must be able to see companies held accountable.

It wasn't an incident that was a distraction from the actual happenings that take place in Wall Street and Washington. It's clear that the fact these issues were asked will affect how companies behave in the near future.

It's certainly somewhat unfair that Robinhood was singled out during this whole situation because other platforms have done the same thing, however, it's likely that Robinhood was the one to do the most damage.

The question of liquidity was brought up. Robinhood did not provide an affirmative answer on whether they deceived investors by saying they didn't have an issue with liquidity but then attempting to raise funds and stop buying since they couldn't afford to provide any additional collateral (CNET 2021).

The House Committee on Financial Services was also interested in knowing whether Griffin was involved in the Robinhood decision to prohibit trading. He dispelled the idea that he was unaware about the restrictions of Robinhood until they were implemented (Ponciano 2021b).

Gabriel Plotkin was asked if you believe that Elon Musk was the one to start the GameStop fanfare by tweeting "Gamestonk!" He didn't think it was a good idea to speculate on the matter. The reason he did not respond is something of a mystery. I'm guessing there's nothing to gain by slandering billionaires when you're involved in this industry (Ponciano 2021b).

Concerning Keith Gill's Testimony

This isn't so much about a subject that was discussed during the hearing, rather it simply a comment.

Gill is the subject of a class-action suit. The lawsuit claims that Gill pretend to be an investor for the purpose of boost the sales at GameStop but, in reality the fact was that he was not. In the past Gill has been certified and is employed by MassMutual's MML Investors as a financial director (Ponciano 2021a, Ponciano).

The suit further claims Gill claimed that the big hedge funds were bad powerful, big-named, powerful who put Gill in the role of the little guy even though the reality was that he wasn't.

It the plaintiff is Christian Iovin, who used $200,000 as collateral to purchase call options at GameStop as he believed the stock to fall (Ponciano 2021a). We've seen that the stock increased by more than doubling. In essence, the investor lost a significant amount of money.

Gill is in fact an authorized security professional. Gill should have made this clear. MassMutual is also listed in the lawsuit as an accused.

This is the reason why that, when Gill was speaking before the House Committee on Financial Services Gill said that the notion that he was the one to cause the market panic is absurd. He also clarified that his YouTube channel was intended for education only. Gill says he's not seeking to offer anyone any investment guidance, but it's difficult to believe that he is that foolish. If that's his intention, his fans will likely follow him. That's the way social media works. I'm sure that he recognized the power he had.

Gill was in his own way was also a victim of market manipulation since there's a feeling that he initiated the entire GameStop fandom through his posts to YouTube, Reddit, and TikTok.

The opening statement was designed to distance himself from the allegations and counter the claim. It's among the many things you can see the defendant doing in the hearing, presenting himself as a tin-man who invests in risky investments which isn't for everyone. There's a certain real truth to this, but there's also the impression that the man was reckless, particularly being a professional with a license.

However it is true that the Internet can be a source of creating a world completely on its own. he did not have the same control over the events which resulted. The idea of blaming him for that chaotic week is unfair considering that there were many variables at play, some of them well-known, others of them undiscovered and a few that we could not even imagine.

Chapter 11: Stocks And The Stock Market

This chapter provides details on trading in stocks, which includes short and long-term selling and buying, an overview of the analysis of equity and the highlights of squeezes that have occurred in the past , which influenced the MOASS belief for GME as well as other stock like AMC. As investors, it's essential to be able to locate information about corporates and the way in which stocks are valued. Reddit does a great job of this by ensuring that shareholders participate in shareholder meetings, studying corporate documents and helping others learn to vote and take part too. This is happening across the globe with various brokerages. Board chairmen and CEOs are meeting with retail investors in a way that has never been seen before.

Stocks

Publicly traded companies located in the United States such as GameStop (NYSE:GME) provide shares in the open market, which are traded and bought to market players. When you purchase stock it is exchanged for shares of the anticipated future profits for the company. The profits could be derived from capital appreciation, and/or through the payment of dividends. The ownership of shares also grants voting rights . If you hold a substantial stake, you could have the ability to influence corporate strategies like Ryan Cohen did. Be aware of the risks for equity investors since shareholders aren't assured of any returns. If a company goes bankrupt the shareholders who are common to it will be at the bottom of a lengthy line of investors, with bondholders and creditors in the lead. There is a lot of risk involved in the market for stocks However, there is the possibility of making substantial gains. The theory of modern portfolios suggests that there is a connection between the risks of an asset and the amount of return desired by the investors. In other words, the more risky it is the investment, greater the potential return it will be able to earn.

The general rule is that stock prices are affected by various variables ranging from the unique (factors particular to the business like volume, debt load supply and demand, competition corporate governance, and other such factors) to the systemic (broad macroeconomic variables like unemployment, rates of interest GDP, FX rates, and other factors) that can impact the stock market in general, or only the particular sector that which the stock is a part of. However, we have observed the effect of GME that the number of shares available and the actions of short sellers may also affect the price of the stock. Retail buyers who are rushing in to boost the stock in the wake of algorithmic trades made by hedge funds that are looking for trends may cause a stock to rise up. If there isn't much volume or no volume, the stock could stall or trade in a tepid manner. Before we proceed it is important to be talking about the conventional methods for valuing equity in order to assist to determine if GME's price GME as well as any other stocks is reasonable. Traditional valuations should at the very least serve as some benchmarks, however the value of any company is what it believes it is. And according to the saying that the market will never be right.

A brief overview of Traditional Equity Analysis

What is a fair value for a company like GME? What factors affect the price? Are the values we get from the market accurate? What are the ways to assess the riskiness of an investment? While prices are often discovered on the market There are a few methods we can use to evaluate the price of an asset. In essence, prices are driven by the expectation of future earnings, therefore the current price is calculated as an estimate of the discount cash flow the expected future earnings. Based on Benjamin Graham, who is often referred to as to be the "dean of analysis in finance" and the "father of value investing,"" the earnings capacity of an organization is the primary basis for value. Therefore, in order to value any stock, it is essential to know the its present and future growth potential. (For more on the father of Graham look up Security Analysis, the classic 1934 book that Graham co-authored along with David Dodd and is still popular today.)

Also, we must consider the inherent risk inherent to an asset. This risk is built into the cost of the asset, which is reflected in the proper selection in discount rates. The best way to select this discount rate is a subject of debate and debate that continues to be debated even today. There is a whole section on risk in the book the moment we'll divide risk associated with equity into two categories that are systematic risk that all stocks are exposed to, and unsystematic risk (or the idiosyncratic risk) which is the particular company's portion of risk.

The ideal scenario is for the analyst to create a model of the company's financial statements such as the balance sheet , and cashflow statement and then run scenarios. We won't get deep into this however it is the most effective way to comprehend the effect of the various variables. Instead, we'll examine a few multiples and basic models like The dividend discount model Gordon Growth Model and others which can serve as quick estimates of stock value.

In addition, meme stocks such as GME as well as AMC are new to the market and could alter the fundamental analysis of equity for ever. A number of banks have abandoned the idea and stopped covering them because there's no explanation for their worth beyond the fact meme stocks are popular and that everyone loves them. It is useful to be aware about the fundamental analysis of equity.

Effective market theory

In the beginning, we will introduce our efficient market hypothesis (EMH) Also known as"the random walk" theory that is a concept of how prices are determined in the market . It is the basis of the modern portfolio theory. The EMH theory states that prices in the future will be random. While future prices may follow a certain path that is linked to expected growth in corporate earnings, they can fluctuate depending on random events. There are three different levels of the efficient market hypothesis The weak form and the semi-strong and the stronger form. (In the instance of GameStop We do not have all the details about the stock, however the retail customers are aware of more about this stock than ever prior to.)

The weak version of the EMH affirms that security prices are a compilation of the entire publicly accessible trading data including volume of trading, price per share as well as short-interest. This means that studies of price history don't contain information that can aid in predicting the future price, therefore charting and other methods of technical analysis will not perform. (The notion in this case is that since the information is freely available that all investors have access to it and this information is considered in the security price.)

The semi-strong version of the EMH claims that security prices are a part of every trading information known along with the company's fundamentals. Therefore, no significant price trend can be predicted through the formation of relations between accounting variables, such as dividends/shares, earnings/share and various financial ratios. (The idea behind this is similar to the weaker form: such information is easily available from websites such as Bloomberg.com which is why it could already be present in the cost for the securities.)

The strongest form of EMH claims that prices for security reflect all the information that is possible to obtain about a firm including private and public and includes the trading variables, all financial data, and other information accessible only to insiders. The only factor that can affect the value of a security is the emergence of new information that enters the market at random and is not known. In this case price movements are determined by random walks. The strong form is comprised of the weak form , as and the semi-strong version as illustrated below.

How to Assess the Value of a Business

If we are trying to figure out the extent to which a business is under- or overvalued it is possible to calculate its value by ourselves with the help of the methods and theorems that are part of Equity Analysis.

We will also discover that the value of a meme's stock is a lot more challenging, especially for companies like GameStop the story of transformation creates a premium or perhaps memium that we'll have to determine.

The three most popular ways to assess the value of a business are:

Discounted Cash Flow (DCF)

Assessing a business using DCF will be one of the more thorough and time-consuming of analysis techniques available. But, once the model is built it will give an excellent grasp of the assumptions as well as important factors that drive value to a company and be able to run stress simulations.

The principle behind this is that the worth of a business is equal to the value of the expected future cash flows which will be paid out to investors. Investors include debt holders, preferred dividend holders , and the common equity holders. In order to determine the value of the ordinary stock we have to use cash flows which are expected to go to common shareholders .

It starts with an analysis of the financial statements of the company including the balance sheet, income statement and statements of the flow of money. These should be examined in relation to the management's outlook strategy, as well as the performance of the board and management. Estimates of the market's growth rate as well as the mix of products and volumes as well as liabilities, the possibility of debt repayment, and more are incorporated to forecast your financial statement and to discount the cash flows up to the present. If, following this, you find an amount that is greater than the market value it could be that you have found the value of a stock.

A fundamental DCF model involves forecasting the free cash flows for the company for a specified time period and then discounting these cash flows at WACC, which is the weighted average of cost (WACC). The business's capital structure includes capital that is provided by shareholders and debt holders. So, WACC is computed as the percentage of capital invested in equity multiplied by the expense of capital equity, plus the amount of debt-related capital multiplied by tax-adjusted interest cost of the debt .

The cost of equity capital is calculated using the Capital Asset Pricing Model (CAPM) while the cost of debt is calculated from the interest that is charged to each line of debt.

The CAPM model is linear modeling that connects the return on an excess from an equity securities (such such as GME) in relation to the extra returns of markets. The principle is that security risk is accounted for by a variable known as beta. It is believed investors should be compensated for the risk and the higher the risk, higher the return that an investor will be able to get. The formula used to calculate CAPM is: CAPM is:

In terms of the excess returns,

Where

Rs = the return on securityand percent

Rf = risk-free rate percent

Rm = Return on Market portfolio and %

= measure of the correlation between security portfolios and market securities

The CAPM is a method to calculate the necessary yield on equity capital required to be included in the valuation of a security (it is the most appropriate discount rate) or to assess the an investment's relative attractiveness. The legitimacy that the CAPM is a hot topic of academic debate, along with concerns like what should be considered the appropriate risk-free rate, what type of market portfolio should be utilized to determine if a market-based portfolio exists, if beta stays stable over time and whether beta is still alive or dead.

Computing WACC

First, you must use CAPM to calculate the expected return on equity that is not levered equity. Next, use the leveraged return formula to calculate the an expected return on equity that is levered. Then, you can use the company's equity and debt weightings to calculate WACC which is the discount rate used to evaluate the company. Then, you can adjust the company's specific WACC according to similar valuations of companies.

Note This is because the CAPM is a requirement for that the firm's equity beta be which for GME is approximately -1.96 as of the date of this writing. The equity beta may be negative, but this signifies it is possible that GME is twice as volatile as the base market and it moves to the contrary. But this renders the calculation of capital cost using CAPM difficult. I suggest that the beta's absolute value be considered. For GME in the above scenario, assuming the market returns are 5percent as well as the risk-free percentage is one percent, the return required on GME will be

An example calculation for WACC:

Let's say a company has a capital of $100 million and of that $40 million is debt and the remaining $60 million of equity. The amount of debt costs 8 percent and equity costs are 12percent. Corporate tax rates are 25 25%.

Then, the

Cash flow that is free (FCF) is typically described as:

Operating Income (also called EBIT[90Operating Income (also known as EBIT[90]) * (1-Tax Rate)

In addition: Amortization and Depreciation (or other non-cash charges)

Lower as a change in the Net Working Capital as well as Capital Expension

Typically, you'll estimate a FCF value for every year for a specific time frame (usually five or 10 year) and then include an end-of-life value (TV) on behalf of the company. The TV is a representation of the firm as a perpetuity that is growing and is a representation of the value that extends beyond the time horizon of the forecast. There are a variety of theories regarding televisions that are computerized, most important ones are:

1.) If you assume that growth is perpetual by using CF/(r-g) or the Final year FCF

(1+g)/(k-g) then discount it until you get the present price (PV).

2.) Make use of the P/E ratio multiplied by Nth year earnings, and then reduce it to calculate PV.

3.) Utilize the Market-Book ratio of similar businesses and reduce it to PV.

4.) Utilize an Exit Multiple based upon EBIT or EBITDA

The FCFs and TVs are then discounted to the WACC. This is referred to as"the" Enterprise Value. When you subtract net debt (debt that is not in cash) and cash, you're leaving with an equity amount for your business. A value of equity divided by the amount of dilute shares in circulation is the share value.

More on Enterprise Value here.

Trading Comparables (Comps)

Another method of valuing the company is to find similar (this isn't always easy) companies similar to the one you wish to assess and then determining the value they trade at various aspects. For instance, if the comparable companies have a value between 5x and 10x EBIT and the one I am valuing is worth an EBIT of $19 million (GME as on 1/31/2021) and so on, then the use of this comparison would place GameStop in a range of the $95 million and 190 million dollars. With approximately 65 million shares in circulation that would put the value of GameStop as a range of $1.46 to $2.92/share. But this isn't the full story, since GameStop is changing itself and it's difficult to locate a comparable competitor.

Acquisition Comparables

They're similar to Trading Comps. If similar companies were bought for 5x-10x profits and GameStop (for instance) has 100 million in revenue and this number could mean it that GameStop might be valued anything between $500 million and $1 billion dollars.

The key to a comparable valuation is identifying the appropriate group of comparables. Of course, choosing companies that are in the same field is essential however, it is also important to consider other elements like the structure of capital (companies that leverage more could trade differently from companies who use equity financing in all forms) and size, seasonality as well as operating margins.

Other methods of valuation include liquidation value and leveraged Buy-Out.

Because reading through this would constitute an entire book I'm not going to go into detail in this moment however if you'd like to know more about this subject, there are a few resources on my blog in the heading of Equity Research.

Instead, we'll explore simple ratios and models to evaluate the value GameStop.

This is the Dividend Discount Model

The most straightforward model to use could be described as the dividend discount model. We simply predict the dividend stream in the future and discount them by the correct capital cost to determine the present worth of the dividend stream. This is the price of the share. The most basic scenario is when a company pays dividends that is expected to be constant throughout the course of time. This is the situation in a mature firm. The price of the shares is calculated with the perpetuity model

In the formula above, DIV stands for the dividend that is stable. It is the price of equity capital that isn't visible. One method to calculate it is to apply the Capital Asset Price Model. Another method is to inquire from management about what their hurdle rates for future projects. (Hurdle rate refers to the minimum amount of return they must receive prior to making an investment in something. It can also be called the rate of return that is required.)

It is easy to see the shortcomings in the assumptions of this model of dividend discounts in just a few minutes by looking at GameStop. GME was a dividend payer however, they stopped doing so in June of 2019. It's a major decision for a business to take however it is a necessary step for the survival of the business. It was announced at the time that was reported the following "The company announced in conjunction with its results for the first quarter that it would be eliminating its quarterly dividend immediately. The $0.38 per-share dividend, that yields dividends of more than 20% will no longer be paid. The move will free the company of $157 million per year which can help the company reduce its debt."[91Thus, the value calculated using the model of perpetual dividend should be treated with a shaker of salt. But, it could serve as a benchmark or to gauge what the market is going to be like.

Example: Let's suppose that GME begins paying its dividends again. When the dividend for 2017 is 4*0.38 is $1.52 and the costs of capital equity is 15 percent, then what would the value for the shares be according to this dividend discount formula?

Question: If shareholders anticipate to receive a continuous flow of $1.520 dividends and the price for equity capital will be constant the answer is yes.

Gordon growth model Gordon growth model

When the payout is projected to continue growing with a constant rate of growth g, the price of the stock will be greater than that is calculated above. In this scenario the value of the share is determined by using the formula

The primary driver behind the pricing in this particular model comes from the difference between costs of capital equity and rate of growth that the dividend. However, we'll need to calculate the rate of growth that the dividend pays, and this must be in some degree correlated with the growth of the business and, as we've learned that companies don't expand in perpetuity. A model such as this could be used to determine the market's expected growth rate however.

Example: What price would GME's be if its dividend was projected to increase by 10% per year?

How did these models fare in determining the price of GME? Because the cost is currently $175, there must be something these models aren't capturing. This is why the Gordon growth model should be used with caution. If the rate of growth exceeds what equity capital costs, then a lower value per share could result. A business cannot expand at a rapid rate for an indefinite amount of time because otherwise it could overtake the entire economy. We can develop more sophisticated dividend discount models that take into account companies that may have varying rate of growth over the course of time. (For example, we might apply this method when a high-tech company grows rapidly over some time, and then enters an in-between period when sales may start to stabilize before entering an older period of steady growth. These models include but include but are not limited to models for dividends with two stages the H Model and the three-stage dividend discount model.)

These models also can be used for companies that pay dividends or are likely to pay dividends in the near future. Therefore, they aren't able to be used to assess startups and other businesses that don't pay dividends like GME. For these companies it is possible to use multiples analysis to determine the value.

Multiples Analysis

Common multiples in valuation are price/earnings, price/sales dividend/price, as well as market value/book values. While multiples are straightforward to employ, we need to be cautious because we aren't sure what is the "right" number is. To evaluate a company by using a multiple will require an array of "comparable" companies to compare. Furthermore, because the lack of understanding or understanding about the company's fundamentals or outlook is required to employ the multiples approach analysis, multiples, if not properly used, can result in misleading price estimates. However, let's test some of these ratios using GME.

Ratio of earnings/price

The "earnings" here refers to Net income per share. Net income is utilized because it's theoretically the money that can be paid to investors. Net income is the amount of income less from operating costs, tax, and the capital for debt that has been negotiated to be paid. Because net income is reported each quarter (at minimum in U.S. companies), it is necessary to report historical also known as "trailing" earnings. GME has negative earnings because its operating expenses were higher than its gross profit at the latest report (Q1 2021) thus let us take the Q4 of 2018 for an illustration.

Let's suppose that the median number of shares owned over the course of the quarter was 101.3 million. The net profit for the quarter was 34.7 million. Earnings/share is $34.7 million/101.3 millions shares equals $0.3425/share. If price/share was $12.62, then price/earnings = (price/share)/(earnings/share) = $12.62/$0.3425= 36.85.

While the ratio of P/E cannot be calculated if there is negative income and yahoo finance actually displays N/A for P/E in the trailing period however, we can calculate an forward P/E, which currently is 36.76. This is a lot however it is not unreasonable. It is possible to compare this with other companies within GameStop's industry that is Consumer Cyclicals, Other Specialty Retailers. To help us understand, we'll look at AMZN with a P/E ratio of 60.16. Sony Corporation Sony Corporation has a PE ratio of 11.55.

The multiples are used for comparison with other stocks or indices to determine the relative value or the appeal of the stock or to determine the prices when other metrics aren't available.

If we want to determine the value of an identical company to GME We could use this ratio. Let's say the comparable company has earnings per share of $1.50. The price will be determined by the formula: 36.76($1.50) is $55.14. This is possible even if the business does not have plans to pay dividends.

Enterprise Value

A different approach to the Price/Earnings ratio can be Enterprise Value. Value could be defined in terms of value for the business as an entity and is thought to be more valuable than looking to the price. The Enterprise Value is the price that an investor would be willing to be willing to pay for the whole company. If you're thinking whether market capitalization is an accurate indicator of the value of a company it is not. Market capitalization is missing a lot of key elements, including the company's cash reserves, its debt and other factors. Enterprise value is considered as a variation of market capitalization since it includes cash and debt in determining the valuation of a business.

The value of the enterprise for GME is $21.09 billion [92at the time on the 9th of June, 2021, with the market cap of 22.29B. The value of the enterprise can be used to calculate financial ratios, such as EBITDA/EV, EV/EBIT, EV/Revenues and more.

EBITDA is an income statement that indicates Earnings before Interest and Taxes and Amortization. EBIT is used as we want to determine the earnings potential of a business. Because interest is paid using pre-tax dollars, the company's capacity to pay interest at a current rate does not affect taxation. However, there are some shortcomings with the use of EBIT The reasons are: 1.) Interest isn't an all-in, fixed cost or expense. (2) EBIT does not provide all cash flows that can be used to service debt, especially when a company has high amortization and/or depreciation costs.

EBITDA can be useful to short-term lenders like banks, who might not want for corporate lenders to make loans (other than real-estate-backed loans) for extended time frames. Since depreciation-generated funds can be used to service debt, EBITDA may be useful. In the moment, GME has negative earnings and this number must be kept in reserve until when it is more appropriate.

Dividend Yield

When GME paid dividends The dividend yield was calculated by dividing the dividend/price ratio which is $1.52/$12.62 = 1.204 percent. If the yield on dividends and dividend is established, it is possible to determine the prices. (Hopefully, GME will start paying dividends in the near future, but as an investor, I'm satisfied to see GME invest in expansion this moment and that dividends will be held off.)

Research has been conducted on the ability to forecast its dividend rate of S&P500 and other indices for forecasting the tops and bottoms of markets.

A very high dividend yield indicates it is a sign that markets are overvalued and a lower yield indicates it is overvalued. If the mean-reversion theory holds this means that times of low yields will be followed by lower prices. However, nobody can pinpoint exactly when this happens since dividends are volatile and averaging out, this indicator might not be as useful as it was before. But, there is an inverted relationship between payout rate of dividends and S&P 500 level and the most recent data could suggest it is close to its maximum.

Price/sales

The ratio of sales to price is commonly used as sales are the sole source of net earnings and, consequently, dividends can be paid. Furthermore, sales are believed to be less susceptible to manipulation in accounting than earnings, meaning that the ratio may remain steady as time passes. This price-to-sales (P/S) ratio is employed for businesses who do not yet have earnings reported like start-ups or ones that have negative earnings, like GME currently.

GME's P/S stood at 4.1 at the time of writing 1/31/2021 and the trailing 12-month sales of $5.0898 billion. The market value would be calculated using the formula of multiplying P/S by S, resulting in $20.8618 billion. In the event that there were 65.3 million shares in circulation and using P/S to calculate the price of shares results at a cost of around $319 per share. The ratio of P/S could be a suitable metric for GME even though the company does not pay dividends. As we've already mentioned the net income that is that shareholders can access is negative because the sales' gross profit isn't enough to cover operating costs this is the reason the business must maintain its growth.

Book value/price

A price-to-book value (P/BV) ratio offers an analysis of current value of a company's stock with their book value for each share. The idea behind this is that the business should be able to make use of its assets to earn profits. For GME the book value/price ratio in the last quarter was 29.27. The book or equity value, is calculated by subtracting liabilities from assets. It is obtainable by examining the balance sheet of a business. This is the amount that remains to be given to shareholders. In the case that book value is 6.69 it would be an average share price of price/book value * share value equals 29.27*6.69 is $195.8163. Share value has been decreasing over time, but it has been increasing in recent times.

The problem with the ratio of P/BV is certain assets, like marketable and cash-flowing securities are recorded at market prices and longer-term assets are recorded at the historical cost of acquisition. This could lower book value, and also overstate the ratio of P/BV in many situations. For many companies that are service-oriented like consulting or software companies, assets are the talent of employees which is not recorded in the balance sheet. This means that book value may appear low. Companies that provide services might have higher ratios of P/BV because they own fewer tangible assets (land buildings, equipment and construction). Companies that are growing and making significant capital expenditures may have lower ratios for P/BV however, as the assets begin to decrease in value and the ratio will be increasing.

Cash flow and price

This ratio is a measure of comparing a company's share price with the free cash flow it generates per share. Free cash flow is the amount that is due to common shareholders following any capital expense or interest payment has been paid, as well as any preferred dividends are paid. By using accounting statements the free cash flow could be established. Because it's more likely for businesses to alter the actual flow of cash as opposed to earnings, the price for cash flow could be a better gauge of earnings capability as opposed to the P/E percentage.

For GME the most recent price to cash flow free value is 69.86. Be aware that these measures are dependent on the stock's price and since GME's price is volatile, any measure based on price is also volatile.

For contrast to the free cash flow price of AMZN stood at 31.9 as well as 9.57 in the case of AAPL.

Short Selling

We discussed the possibility of buying the stock as well as the factors which influence its price. One of the main reasons for the focus on GME along with other"meme stocks" like Reddit "meme stock" like Bed, Bath and Beyond, AMC, Nokia, Blackberry and many others was the fact that many saw huge short positions [93] in GameStop.

Short selling an investment (or simply "shorting") could be an approach that is employed when a trader thinks that a stock's price is likely to fall in the near future. If the owner already owns shares, then they may declare this belief by simply selling their shares. They could also consider buying put (covered in the following chapter) to cover the risk and then keep the stock. What happens if you don't own the stock but want to gain from any potential downside? Short selling is the selling of a share that the investor doesn't currently have. It's like this:

1.) Short sellers, which could represent a hedge funds investor or retail investor, takes the shares from their broker in exchange for the agreement to return the shares in the future.

2.) A short-seller will sell the stock at the market price.

3.) A short-seller is subject to interest when they borrow the stocks. Retail investors could get this kind of interest if their brokerage lends them shares.

4.) At some time, the short seller must cover their position, which means them to purchase the shares on the market in the open and return the shares back to the broker they dealt with.

5.) When the value has dropped and they are able to make profit. When the value has mostly traded in a range of 0 to 100 but they still pay short interest. If the price hasn't declined or been increasing in the past, the short seller must soon realize there's too much pain that comes with keeping the position. They will take the shares back at a greater price in order to end the position.

The Financial Times provided the following graphic that illustrates the short selling process in their January 29, 2021 story "GameStop's wild Ride How Reddit traders created a'short squeeze'"

A lot of people have been hurt extremely badly through short selling of stocks, even hedge fund professionals with sophisticated skills like Melvin Capital. Others have also made money. GameStop is unique because of the fact the sense that retailers fought back and continued to purchase the shares, causing a number of hedge funds to rack up massive losses and regulators to be forced to take note and propose new regulations on trading in shorts and the transparency.

To be able to sell a stock short there must be enough stock to lend. Retailers are trying to keep hold of their shares (or diamond-hand them) The theory is that the cost will need to rise as short sellers eventually have to take on.

One of the problems in GME as well as other shares that are sold for short sale is that it isn't accurate, real-time information about the quantity of shares that were sold short or who is responsible for the selling. If there are a small number of shares to be repurchased to finish this short position, then a phenomenon called short squeeze could occur.

After reading financial reports and government filings and redditors as and others noticed the fact that more GME shares that were sold short than could be found on the market. They also began discussing a possible MOASS or Mother Of All Short Squeezes which might eventually happen.

A MOASS was anticipated because reports of short interest indicated that over 100 percent of shares available were shorted. If this is the case, and shares need to be bought in the future, prices for shares will be soaring as demand surpasses supply. As of May 20, 2021 the date isn't certain if the short squeeze has actually taken place and if it has, but GameStop's GameStop Twitter account seems to be enjoying the possibility of an MOASS that could take prices to the moon , or above. For instance On the 11th of May, 2021, the GameStop account shared the image of an astronaut sipping beers on the moon wearing GS (for GameStop) on his space suit with the words "Been gone for the past few months. What have I missed?" (However, I think the astronaut should be eating the delicious AMC Chicken tenders!)

GameStop made an explicit reference to the anticipation of a massive short squeeze, when it tweeted "Oops My mistake" in response to a trailer of the upcoming game titled "Mass Effect: Legendary Edition". The companies aren't happy with those who sell their stock short . A couple of examples are provided below.

Historical Short Squeezes , Market Corners

In generally short squeezes occur when a stock heavily shorted is pushed up sharply, forcing short sellers to sell their short positions, which contributes to the pressure to climb to the share price. Short sellers aren't necessarily bad. In many cases, the expression of a negative opinion about the stock is not necessarily true however, some stocks are overvalued, like the well-known New Jersey deli trading under the ticker HWIN that is worth close to $100 million. However, due to 80.46 percent of the shares held by insiders there are no shares for shorting.

Short squeezes may also happen in situations where there are a limited number of shares in the market. A good example would be HWIN above, in the event that it was possible to short the stock.

Sometimes instead of selling shares, traders try to raise the price by taking over the market. This is done by quietly purchasing massive shares, and then requesting an astronomical price to anyone who wants to buy them.

If you want to find stocks that have the potential to be subject to short squeezes then you should check the short interest as well as the short-interest ratio. Short interest provides the amount of shares sold short, as a percent of the number of shares outstanding. The short interest is calculated by the total amount of short-sold shares divided by the average daily trading volume for the stock. It is difficult to determine the amount of shares that are sold short however. For investors with retail accounts These numbers are announced twice a week by FINRA and the exchanges on which the shares trade on, which means they are outdated when they are published.

Some of the most well-known instances of short squeezes and market corners are described below. It's fascinating to examine these cases and how they were eventually resolved. they may have parallels with GME.

The Silver Squeeze

The rate of inflation was extremely extreme in United States in the 1970s. It was the Hunt Brothers, heirs to huge fortunes, saw the situation and began looking for ways to make money from the growing inflation, despite the diminishing buying capacity for the dollars. They thought about buying gold bullion (a usual hedge against inflation) however, it was expensive. Silver prices are strongly dependent on gold. In the graph below, the cost of gold is displayed on the left and silver shown on the other.

With silver being much cheaper than gold The Hunt brothers set out to take advantage of the market for silver by buying silver at a low cost and also purchasing futures contracts. In the wake of their efforts, the price of silver went up from $11 to over $50 an ounce. This price rise was noticed by other traders, who responded by selling short silver futures. Brothers continued to buy silver futures. When prices began to climb upwards, short sellers began to cover their positions, purchasing back silver at any price they could. The purchases pushed the cost of silver up, eventually to $63/ounce, which attracted new buyers for silver.

The drama ended when regulators came in. Rules that banned trading of long position the silver market were put in the market. These rules , along with the massive short selling actions resulted in the price falling. The brothers started receiving phone calls from brokers requesting margin. Their credit lines started to run dry and, on the 27th of March 1980, also known as "Silver Thursday," the Hunt brothers could not meet the margin requirements. The news spread and caused a panic selling. The price of silver eventually dropped to $11/ounce.

The Copper Squeeze

In the aftermath of the silver squeeze the copper trader with Sumitomo Copper caused a $1.8 billion loss, which had accrued over the preceding ten years. The chief copper trader of the company, Yasuo Hamanaka, had been trying to make money by controlling the market for copper.

Hamanaka was known as "Mr. 5%" (or "Mr. Copper") as the amount of his trades, which was 500,000 tonnes, represented five percent of the annual global amount of 10 millions metric tonnes. The report said that Hamanaka could conceal the losses he suffered, the very least partially, due to the fact that he utilized the forwards market rather than the futures market for his long-term positions. Since forwards do not have to be traded daily, whereas futures do, he did not need to disclose his profit and loss. Futures trading could have led the company to the issue earlier.

Hamanaka was able arrange for extended settlement dates with his trading counterparties they relied on Sumitomo's credibility. Because a variety of traders were competing to control of the markets for copper and Sumitomo's increasing accumulation in copper did not get scrutinized by market watchers who believed that Sumitomo was trying to squeeze competitors.

As soon as Hamanaka's trading behavior was made public the market was able to predict that Sumitomo would restructure his vast copper portfolio and a panic selling ensued.

In the final phase, Hamanaka was fired, and the de-winding of his tenure impacted the entire market for copper which caused copper prices to drop from a record high of $2,658 per metric tonne in May 1996, to an almost two year low of $1,935 a tonnes September 1, 1996.

The New York Times reported that:

"The selling of copper was due to an article published in The Financial Times of London on Saturday, which reported that Sumitomo could have as much as 2.2 million tonnes of copper that it could sell .... Investors are all worried about the Hamanaka impact according to Michael Frawley, a vice president of Dean Witter Reynolds Inc. in New York. "I'm shocked that Sumitomo is still 2 million tons long. No one is able to hide the amount of copper that's in there however, investors aren't willing to gamble with their money.'" [96]

The tale ended in the same way that a lot of these stories end in the form of the possibility of fines, lawsuits, and even prison.

Sumitomo ended up suffering $2.6 billion loss due to Hamanaka's trading, and an additional $200 million USD arising from subsequent lawsuits regarding the incident. [97 A Tokyo court has found Hamanaka guilty of fraud and forgery in 1997, and sentenced the defendant to eight years' prison.

Volkswagen

Volkswagen AG is a German automaker with its headquarters in Frankfurt and listed in the Frankfurt Stock Exchange. On July 28, 1960, the company was taken private and a law, "Gesetz uber die Uberfuhrung der Anteilsrechte an der Volkswagenwerk Gesellschaft mit beschrankter Haftung in private Hand", or "VW-Gesetz" for short, was enacted, which was intended to protect Volkswagen against hostile takeovers. The law stipulated it was a condition that nobody Volkswagen AG shareholder would be permitted to have more than 20% of the company's voting rights, regardless of the amount of stock they owned. At the time, 20.2% of the voting shares of the company were owned by the state from Lower Saxony, a state located in Northern Germany. The voting rights granted to the state with the ability to block important decisions and to block the taking over of other shareholders.

Porsche began to acquire shares of Volkswagen which was their largest partner. They purchased the 18.53 percentage stake the month of October 2005. This was increased to over 25% in July. It was the

Volkswagen law was overturned in 2007. Following the EU protested against VW-Gesetz Porsche increased its stake into Volkswagen to 30.9 percent. The number of shares was an offer to buy Volkswagen under German law [98] that describes takeovers as bids that are aimed at controlling that is, control means the possession of at least 30 percent in voting rights of the company you want to buy.

Porsche said it didn't intend to takeover, but was accumulating its stake to limit anyone else who wanted to take the largest stake. Additionally, they wanted to ward off the possibility of hedge funds taking control and eventually destroying Volkswagen. Porsche declared that it did not intend to increase its stakes to 75%. Porsche stated that "In considering it is the case that Lower Saxony as second largest shareholder holds 20% of VW and the likelihood of getting the shares from the free float is very low." Since the price of VW rose the short sellers began to take positions.

On the 16th of September, the 16th of September, 2008 Porsche revealed that it had now control of 35 percent of Volkswagen and that , as of October, it had actually held 74.1 percent of the company. This consisted of 42.6 percent in common shares, and convertible options on 31.5 percent of the stock. This means that 94.3 percent of the shares were owned by Porsche and the state in Lower Saxony, which caused panic among short sellers, who purchased shares, which caused the price to nearly quadruple from 220 euros to over 1000 euros in a two-day period. This led to Volkswagen being the biggest corporation in terms of market capitalization world. A lot of short sellers lost significant amounts of money. Unfortunately, German billionaire Adolf Merkle was in the wrong place trading and lost an estimated 400 million euros. He then took his own life in 2009. The New York Times noted that:

"One of the most significant risk associated with the herd-mind strategy for shorting is lots of money could be made at the beginning," Ed Oliver, an executive business consultant at Spitalfields Advisors, a London-based firm that is specialized in securities lending and advising on securities lending, told Bloomberg News. "But it is possible to lose all of it if you attempt to end the position. There's no limit."

The aftermath Volkswagen took over Porsche on July 12, 2012, which resulted in the merger of the firm Porsche AG that became the 10th Volkswagen brand.

For more details, check out VW Briefly rivals Exxon for the Biggest Cap in Market Cap (cnbc.com) as well also As GameStop falls the stock of Volkswagen's short squeeze in 2008 provides an indication of how difficult it could become (cnbc.com)

The Volkswagen scandal is used to provide a comparison to the soaring of the share prices of GameStop. This analysis is made available by CNBC[99[99].

Herbalife

in 2012 Pershing Square hedge fund manager Bill Ackman bet $1 billion against the nutritional supplement manufacturer Herbalife which he claimed was an illegal pyramid scheme where the distributors for its shakes as well as other products made more money by bringing new recruits to the network rather than selling, which is a multi-level marketing strategy but Herbalife claims that it is not an illegal pyramid scheme. The hedge fund manager made a deal to sell 20 million shares in short which is approximately 56% of the shares short sold according to the January 15 data published by Nasdaq. In a unique twist it was that he borrowed cash to purchase the shares to reduce the additional possibility of margin calls that could lead to the closing of a trade or the sale of stocks that would take care of. The shares plummeted 40 percent following the speech.

According to the Financial Post observed that "Ackman could be able to stand firm on his conviction that Herbalife is an unregulated pyramid scheme which earns the bulk of its profits through the sales it makes to its network of distributors, not from consumers. However, it may take years before his opinion pans out, if at all it does, setting the stage for a long-running battle with Herbalife's most bullish investors.

A brief rout in the stock started after the Third Point hedge fund announced that it had accumulated an equity stake of 8 percent in Herbalife which took place from December 24 through January 15, during which time the price of the stock soared between $26.06 to $46.19 up 77.

The famous shareholder activist Carl Icahn also bought shares. Icahn and Ackman had a heated argument in the early days, slandering one another in the media.

"Less less than one week following the announcement of Ackman on December 20th We saw a significant rise in the number of traders who covered the short position, presumably which led to a squeeze" explained Karl Loomes, market analyst at SunGard's Astec Analytics, a provider of data on the lending process for securities.

In the course of the short squeeze, it was reported that the price for borrowing Herbalife shares through a broker increased from 1 percent up to a high of 7 percent annually as another sign of the short squeeze.

Ackman continued to fight against Herbalife by switching his short sale strategy to put and finally announcing his resignation from the company on February 28, 2018. The chart above shows it was a wise choice since The stock continued to rise through the year and never dropped below the 2013 low. According to Reuters the wager to Herbalife "turned Ackman into a social activist when he decided to step into a fight against a company that he believed was hurting minority groups with false assurances of financial success, by selling Herbalife.

The U.S. Federal Trade Commission investigated the issue, and ultimately reached an agreement with Herbalife. It included an amount of $200 million in fines as well as a requirement that the business modify its business methods." It was reported that he lost a large portion of the investment of $1 billion and sullied the brand, but not dealing a death blow.

Shares Available

It's obvious that the amount of shares that are available is significant in determining the price and the potential short squeezes, and also the sellers and buyers on both sides, and that have the advantage.

When private businesses go public, they offer shares to institutional and retail investors via An Initial Public Offering (IPO). At this point, the amount of shares that are offered to the public and the cost of the offering are decided. Following the IPO further shares could be sold or purchased through the firm. This directly impacts the number of shares outstanding that is an essential aspect in determining market Capitalization which is also known as the Market Cap (which can be defined as the amount of shares in circulation multiplied by the price of shares.) If there's a limited number of publicly traded shares, there's a possibility of a price hike up if demand for shares rises. For the majority of publicly traded companies that have shares that are outstanding is reported on their website in the section for investor relations and also in their accounts as well as SEC filings. This information is also available on sites such as finance.yahoo.com. For GameStop shares, the outstanding shares can be found on their site in the section on financial information.

statistics

GME Shares Outstanding

On the 6th of March, 2021, the GameStop website indicates that there were 69.75 million shares available with a float that is 54.17 million. Float is the quantity of shares traded on the market for sale and the rest, 15.58 millions of shares remain reserved and are not available for sale to anyone else.

Restricted shares, commonly referred to as Restricted Stock Units or RSUs are usually kept for a certain period of time. These shares can be owned by company founders, investors at the beginning corporate officers, as well as employees. RSUs thus cannot be traded and are not a factor in the amount of outstanding. RSUs are typically offered as a part of a bonus and are considered non-cash compensation. They are offered to employees as a way of encouraging them to keep making the most appropriate decisions to increase the corporate's growth in addition to shareholder benefits. However, RSUs are not traded on the market, when they expire there is a possibility of inside shareholders sell shares, as happened in February, with Palantir (NYSE: The PLTR). Insider sales of shares do not necessarily reflect any deterioration in the company's prospects, it is just that the shareholder was looking for liquidity.

Float is vital, as the amount of shares in the market directly affects the price because it represents the availability. The lower the float, the less availability of stock and the more expensive the possible price, should the price be squeezed by a surge in demand. The bulk of the float is mostly owned by institutional investors, like hedge funds, who are able to take on large positions which is the case with GME. You can discover the names of institutional investors on the GameStop site. GameStop[100] released the following information at the time of February 21st, 2021. It revealed that 27.33 percent of shares held by insiders, with 122.04 percent held by institutions.

The outstanding total is 77.52 percent. However as this data is not updated daily, one may find more recent data on sites such as https://fintel.io/so/us/gme. The site provides data from the forms 13D/G or 13F that are filed with the Securities Exchange Commission (SEC). Based on fintel's data "The schedule 13D signifies that an investor owns (or was holding) more than five percent of the company and plans (or planned) to pursue an active shift in the business strategy. Schedule 13G is an investment that is passive and exceeds five percent."

Fintel says that

"GameStop Corporation. (US:GME) is home to 492 shareholders and owners of institutional ownership who have filed 13D/G and Form 13F for the Securities Exchange Commission (SEC). They hold the total of 110,591,822 shares. The biggest shareholders are Fmr Llc, BlackRock Inc. The FDMLX-Fidelity Series Intrinsic Opportunities Fund Melvin Capital Management LP, Vanguard Group Inc, Senvest Management, LLC, Susquehanna

International Group, Llp, Maverick Capital Ltd, Morgan Stanley and Dimensional Fund Advisors Lp."

The ownership structure for institutions of GameStop company reveals the current positions held by the company owned by funds and institutions and also the most recent modifications to position size. Major shareholders may include private investors as well as mutual funds, hedge funds, or even institutions."

The most influential institutional investors are highlighted below. When 110.591822 million shares have been owned by institutional investors, and there are 69.75 million shares on the market which means that institutional investors hold 158% of the floating. This isn't normal, therefore additional data is needed.

Melvin Capital's Holdings

We also do not have holdings of the hedge fund Melvin Capital, who claimed that they had closed the short position on the 26th of January with a significant loss. It's possible that they are still holding put and calls. To determine this what they have, we should look up the SEC Form 13F[101] that is required for entities holding greater than $100MM to submit various information on an annual basis, which includes the calls as well as puts. The documents are available on Melvin Capital's website, and the SEC's 13F[102] was released on May 17th for their holdings for 2021 through March 31. The 13F must submit within 45 calendar days after the close of a quarter. the file was filed 47 days later, meaning we don't know whether they were still holding puts in January 26 or their positions at the date of filing.

The report for Q1 2021 doesn't reveal no positions from GameStop although they did have positions in 2020. The filing for the last quarter of 2020 shows Melvin Capital held 5,400,000 puts that was down from 6,000,000 put positions in the previous filing. We can confirm that he's had put on GME since at the very least in 2016.

The chart below explains the reasons why the put strategy might be unprofitable. As the price of shares increased, Melvin Capital also increased the number of put options. In fact The Financial Times noted that between the second and the third quarter of the year 2020 Plotkin increased his puts by a third by increasing his put to 3.4 million up to 5.4 million, even though the price of shares had increased by 135 percent. It is also important to note that a 13F file only contains only a portion of the information, and it is impossible to calculate the total short position of a fund or position "Wall Street is still speculating about the exact size the position of Plotkin. The filing (the 13F file) sufficed to give the fund a hint."

The Financial Times also interviewed a long-short hedge fund's manager, Brad Lamensdorf, who said that "All investors should have some sort of procedure to keep track of the market. Price action precedes volume," he said, and the FT noted that the trading background of GameStop showed signs of heavy buying during the months of November and December in 2020. "When you observe this kind of massive sponsorship and an accumulation of stocks is a risky signal for short-sellers."

Why 13F is so important

The hedge funds have a reputation for hiding their business. As we've mentioned previously, they have to adhere to certain regulatory filings. Beyond the belief that GameStop was overvalued, some redditors were looking over the 13Fs. One of the major factors that triggered the GameStop trade was the huge short position placed in the company by a variety of hedge funds, such as Melvin Capital Management. In an article titled "Buried on Reddit The Roots of Melvin Capital's Financial Crisis" Institutional Investor [103reported that

"The Reddit users were able to find Melvin Capital's short on GameStop because it was disclosed in put options listed. Contrary to the majority of short options in the U.S., those bets have to be made public in reports filed with the Securities and Exchange Commission."

On February 16th 2021 Reuters also revealed that Melvin capital increased put options up to 6 million by the end of 2020.

"(Reuters) A hedge fund Melvin Capital Management on Tuesday revealed that it has increased the call option for Class A shares owned by U.S. Video game retailer GameStop Corp to 6 million shares in the quarter that ended December. 31 from 5.4 million shares over the prior quarter.

The announcement - which follows a flood of retail trading that drove GameStop as well as other stocks to extreme heights in January. It also put pressure on hedge funds such as Melvin Capital who had placed bets against it. However, the disclosure is not a reflection of January's actions which occurred when Melvin announced that it had liquidated it GameStop stake."

So, looking through the files is a good method of determining who is purchasing the stock, even though the data is not up-to-date, and won't show purchases with less than five percent.

It's the GameStop short squeeze

Short sellers began to become conscious of the potential in WSB trader, reuters stated that Wall Street began paying to the issue:

"Wall Street has been keeping vigilant eye on WallStreetBets. Thinknum Alternative Data recently built and released a tool that gives investors and hedge funds with a listing of the top-rated stocks on WallStreetBets.

The information would have enabled Melvin Capital to unwind its bets on GameStop before the company's stock went up. Melvin eventually accepted an $2.75 billion cash injection (don't consider it bailout, per Plotkin) which was led by two rival hedge fund Citadel as well as Point72.

At one time the short interest of GameStop was unimaginable at 140 percent -- a situation that Plotkin predicted is unlikely to happen again.

"I believe that investors such as me want to be prone to these kinds of dynamics," he said."

On April 18, 2021 Ortex stated that

"Investors are believed as having lost 930 million from the short position they held in meme stock GameStop (GME.N) along with AMC Entertainment (AMC.N) over the past five days of trading, figures from the financial analytics firm Ortex reported on Tuesday.

Shares of GameStop is at the center of what's known as the "stonks" trade craze in the beginning of this year, have increased by 33% in one week, and the shares of AMC, a cinema operator AMC have increased by 39%..

Ortex stated that there is a short-term interest rate in AMC can be estimated at 18.3 percent of free float as well for GME the figure is to be 21.8 percent of free float.

Yesterday, the short-sellers collectively suffered losses of more than $200 million for both shares, Ortex data shows. GameStop ended the day 13% higher at $180.6 which is the highest value since April 30."

Which shares of GME are in short at any given moment?

Spoiler Alert: the solution to this question isn't widely known to the general public.

Because hedge funds are less than transparent with respect to how they manage their short-term positions, consumers are unable to access real-time information on the number of GME shares GME is short at any point in time. Brokers, prime or discount, that perform the trades need to know.

In 2015 the NYSE demanded to the Securities Exchange Commission (SEC) to "bring light to an opaque and more consequential part of the market for securities." Pensions & Investments reported that "While the largest funds employ brokers to compile the most current data on short-selling however, the rest of us have to wait two weeks to wait for the exchanges to release the final tally of how many of the company's shares are in loan. The SEC requires hedge funds to disclose their long positions regularly however, it does not have similar rule regarding their short positions." From 2020, FINRA demands that firms disclose short interest positions in all accounts of both proprietary and customer for all equity securities two times each month at the time of 6 p.m.

Eastern Time on the second business day following the date of settlement for reporting.

Retail investors and Redditors examine reports published by organizations like S3 Partners, Fintel and others. The closing date for market trading was May 18th, 2021, Fintel states that there were 400,000 shares to be sold. This doesn't include information from other brokers or dark pools , and as such, fintel suggests that this information should not be interpreted as the total amount of shares available for short on the market. A trend chart as well as the latest short interest data can be located on MarketBeat that reports the short-interest rate of 19.88 percent in April 19 and $1.85 billion in short-term sales.

It is also beneficial to study how short-term interest is performing and its failure to give statistics to determine the current short-term position. The site isthesqueezesquoze.com run by an anonymous user has not been updated since May 4, but as of that date, they indicate that the squeeze has not been squoze and that:

"GME stock did not experience any short squeezes during its most recent highest point. It could have had - like, Robinhood - but short interest began to decrease in that time of extremely massive volume.

Today, on February 24 the resignation of the CFO - a sign that Gamestop is committed to Papa Cohen's plans to revive the company has spurred a new buying enthusiasm. Short interest is massive. It appears that meat is back in the menu, guys."

Memium

With all this data We can conclude that the traditional valuation techniques do not reflect actual share prices of meme stocks such as GameStop. In the case of GameStop, the transformation is only beginning, so historical data should not be used to judge the newly transformed business. The company that is being transformed may be more successful than startups, as they have an extremely high growth rate which is why the H-model of earnings could be used. In the case of GameStop it has a reputable customer base, with experienced executives who have a track record of transformation of retail businesses into online shopping. I wouldn't bet on the meme stocks, which are changing not only their business models, but also how financial analysts will evaluate stocks in the future. Memiums is an appropriate term to apply to these stocks to show the increased demand, the anticipated effect of changes and the impact of short-term interest on the retail market.

www.ingramcontent.com/pod-product-compliance
Lightning Source LLC
Chambersburg PA
CBHW071220210326
41597CB00016B/1884